# The Art of Strategic Decision Making:
## *How to Make Tough Decisions Quickly, Intelligently, and Safely*

By Peter Hollins,
Author and Researcher at
petehollins.com

# Table of Contents

## Introduction

During my fourth and final year of college, I was guilty of making some fairly bad decisions.

Some of them are unfit to be public and involve cans of spray paint and silly string, but one of them was about the apartment I shared with my friends.

We had been looking for about two weeks for a new apartment because our current place was starting to show its age and our lease was almost up. We viewed listing after listing and attended a few open houses until I finally couldn't take it anymore. No one could make a decision about anything. It wasn't so much that we needed the place, but I was frustrated and my impatience took over my brain. I took it upon myself to speed up the process and push a decision.

When it was finally down to two apartments, I heavily pushed one of the apartments, and everyone was on board and took my recommendation so they could get back to their busy lives.

At first glance, this sounds like a story about decisiveness and taking charge, but it's really quite the opposite.

One of my roommates had a dog—a little chihuahua named Banana—that was our apartment's mascot. Every other apartment we looked at was completely fine with dogs, but the apartment I chose was most definitely not. I overlooked this crucial factor in my eagerness to be done with the process. We contemplated sneaking him in and out of the building for a year but decided it was not in our best interests.

What ended up happening was that I confessed to our future landlord, and we had to pay an extra one hundred dollars a month. When I say "we" I mean "I" because I footed the bill on account of it being solely my mistake.

The biggest sin I committed in this decision-making gaffe was assuming that I had all the information. I was lazy. I relied upon an assumption and didn't do the legwork to confirm or deny the assumption. I also struggled under the burden of making the decision for two other people (and a dog) and felt stress and anxiety from the pending deadline.

It was a perfect storm for me to miss an important detail that cost me over a one thousand dollars. Decision making isn't necessarily an art form, but there are very specific ways that human beings can make incredibly suboptimal decisions without even knowing.

The consequences of my mistake with the apartment were relatively small, but what if I had been working on a huge deal with international corporations? There wouldn't be any recovering from that. You simply wouldn't be able to approach the deal without safeguards, processes, and double-checking. But we almost never do those things in our daily lives.

So how we can make better and more optimal decisions more frequently and avoid the internal and external traps that hold us back in life? Do we need to draw up a complex decision matrix for every fork in the road we come upon? Thankfully not.

We can do it by diving into the science and psychology of decisions. What has research shown and what does that mean for us? Why are the evolutionary drives that kept us alive harmful to use in this day and age? What are the roles of emotion and logic in decision making, and should they be different?

Most importantly, why do I still order hamburgers even though I need to lose weight?

This book presents a thorough view of the decision-making landscape and teaches you how to make effective and intelligent decisions through a variety of methods, whether you have perfect information or not. What does beating indecision and becoming more confident in my decisions require? That's what lies ahead.

## Chapter 1. The Core of Decisions: You

Decision making is a term that means different things to different people.

I'm not just talking about how people might define it. I'm talking about the wide variance in driving forces behind people's decisions—the *why* of why people do what they do. What compels one person to do X can be the exact thing that compels their next-door neighbor to the opposite of X. You might rate X as your highest priority and determining factor, while your mother might rate X as an instant deal breaker that will bring shame to the family.

Decision making affects us all differently because we are different people. We might be similar superficially—we all wear blue jeans and like showers. We want jobs that make an amount of money that will leave us comfortable, but we don't want to work long hours. We generally like our families and don't wish physical harm to most people. Those are all shallow factors that we are indeed similar in.

One of the first factors to consider in any decision is the motivation behind it. These differ drastically in each individual, whether they realize it or not. Specifically, most of what influences our decisions and everyday actions are subconscious needs and desires that you are probably unaware of.

These are the motivations and reasons that we instinctually act upon yet may not be able to articulate when pressed to clarify. These are what comprise the "gut feelings," "hunches," or flashes of insight that seemingly come from nowhere. It's because we all have different subconscious needs vying for dominance in our head that seek to influence our actions for greater happiness. You may be able to consciously articulate that you want to eat Chinese food tonight, but that's a one-off decision, whereas your subconscious needs create a unique pattern of behavior.

Unsurprisingly, subconscious desires and motivations have been studied heavily by psychologists over the years. For a brief glance, Sigmund Freud and Ivan Pavlov represent some of the most fascinating findings about our subconscious selves that we listen to far more than our conscious thoughts.

Pavlov is generally considered the discoverer of classical conditioning on account of his experiments with his dog. He paired feeding his dog with ringing a bell, and after a few weeks, his dog salivated at only hearing the bell. Of course, the dog was unaware of how he associated the food with the bell—we are similarly controlled and influenced by factors that we don't consciously realize.

Freud popularized the notion that we are ruled by childhood events, and there are three parts to our personalities. They are called the *id*, *ego*, and *superego*, which all have varying motivations that tear us in different directions. Our conscious thoughts are only a result of internal forces at war and who is winning at that particular moment.

If subconscious desires contribute to our decisions more than we previously realized, then it's clear we have to examine the existing models to categorize them. This allows us to understand what our potential range of needs and desires are, so you might be more aware of what you are influenced by and what you ultimately rely upon to make your decisions.

It's an attempt to make the subconscious more conscious; in essence, you are thinking about your thoughts so you can better understand yourself.

The three models of subconscious desires and needs are Maslow's hierarchy of needs, Tony Robbins's matrix of human desires, and the Max-Neef model of fundamental human needs.

## Maslow's Hierarchy of Needs

Abraham Maslow's primary theory is that human beings are a product of a set of basic needs, the deprivation of which is the primary cause of most psychological problems. He encapsulated his findings into a hierarchy, which maps out basic human needs and desires and how they evolve and change throughout life. The important thing is that it's a hierarchy, meaning that some needs cannot be fulfilled until the ones beneath it are. Your location in the hierarchy at any given time is what influences your subconscious needs and desires.

The needs are: physiological needs (such as for food and shelter), safety, love and belonging, esteem, and the final rung, self-actualization. Maslow believed that very fe people reached this final level, and that most of us achieved only part of our full potential.

The hierarchy functions like a ladder. If you aren't able to satisfy your more basic foundational human needs and desires, it is borderline impossible to move forward to the next ladder rung without profound stress and dissatisfaction in life. The higher you are on the ladder, the more of your physical and security needs are taken care of, at which point you start yearning for psychological needs.

To illustrate, let's briefly look at how our needs change from infancy to adulthood. As infants, we don't feel any need for a career or psychological satisfaction. We simply need to rest, be fed, and have shelter over our heads. Feeding and survival are our only real needs and desires (and changing diapers as parents of newborns will tell you).

As we grow from infants into teenagers, simply staying alive and healthy doesn't bring satisfaction. We hunger for interpersonal relationships and social fulfillment. What drives us is to find a feeling of belonging and community. Then, as we mature into young adults, simply having a great group of friends is no longer enough to satisfy us. It feels empty, actually, without an overall sense of life purpose. We don't like to feel aimless and like every day is the same as the one before it.

If, as young adults, we are fortunate enough to be able to provide financial security and stability for ourselves and our families, then our desires and needs can turn outward rather than inward. It's the same reason that people such as Warren Buffett and Bill Gates start participating in philanthropy to make as big an impact as they can on the world. This is not a stage that everyone will reach in their lives, unfortunately.

As you can see, only when you can satisfactorily accomplish one stage can you move on to addressing the next, higher, and more psychologically fulfilling stage. You can't very well be giving all of your money to charity if you don't feel secure in your own basic needs. Simply put, the stages of Maslow's hierarchy of needs are why you feel unsettled and uncomfortable at work if you are at risk of eviction from your apartment. Your apartment represents your more fundamental need for survival and safety, while your work represents a relatively secondary need.

The stages of the hierarchy are as follows— remember that where you are in the hierarchy is what tends to influence your decisions more than you may realize.

**Physiological Fulfillment.** This is easily seen in the daily life of an infant. All that matters to them is that their basic needs for survival are met (i.e. food, water, and shelter). Without security in these aspects, it is difficult for anyone to focus on satisfaction in anything else. It would actually be harmful to them to seek other forms of satisfaction. This is the baseline level of fulfillment that must first be met. This is logical, because nothing else matters to you if you are homeless or starving.

**Safety.** You might call this stage security. If someone's belly is full, they have clothes on their back, and they have a roof over their heads, they need to find a way to ensure that those things continue. They need to have a secure source of income or resources to increase the certainty and longevity of their safety. The first two stages are designed to ensure overall survival. Unfortunately, many people never make it out of these first two stages due to unfortunate circumstances, and you can plainly see why they aren't concerned with fulfilling their potential.

**Love and Belonging.** Now that your survival is ensured, you'll find that it is relatively empty without sharing it with people that you care about. Humans are social creatures, and studies have shown that living in isolation will literally cause insanity and mental instability, no matter how well fed or secure you are. This stage includes relationships with your friends and family and socializing enough so you don't feel that you are failing in your social life.

Of course, this stage is a major sticking point for many people. They are unable to be fulfilled or focus on higher desires because they lack the relationships that create a healthy lifestyle. Isn't it easy to imagine someone who is stuck at a low level of happiness because they don't have any friends?

Once you reach this level, you start living outside of yourself. You start seeking something bigger and higher than yourself, in part because you don't need to account for yourself as much anymore.

**Self-Esteem.** You can have relationships, but are they healthy ones that make you feel confident and supported?

This stage is all about how your interactions with others impact your relationship with yourself. This is an interesting level of needs because it boils down to self-acceptance. You know you have a healthy level of self-esteem when you can accept yourself even if you are misunderstood, or outright disliked, by others.

For you to get to this stage and have a healthy level of self-esteem, you have to have accumulated certain achievements or earned the respect of others. There is strong interplay between how you get along with others and help others and how you feel about yourself.

**Self-Actualization.** The highest level of Maslow's hierarchy is self-actualization. This is when you are able to live for something beyond yourself and your needs. This is where people chase self-fulfillment and find their destinies, so to speak. When people finally have the foundations of a great life, suddenly that is no longer enough for personal satisfaction.

This is the stage people are at when they say they want to find their calling and purpose in life. They now have the luxury to ruminate on these issues, as opposed to worrying about where their next meal will come from. They can focus on a project, idea, or concept that is above their own petty, self-centered concerns. These are people who can set aside their own needs and work for or toward something that is beyond their mundane and self-serving concerns.

Sadly, many of us may never make it to this stage because we haven't fully satisfied the needs of the prior stages. It is a very privileged position to be in and shouldn't be taken for granted.

If you can accurately pinpoint where you fall in this hierarchy, it will let you know immediately what is going on in the background of your decisions. For example, if you are facing eviction, many of your actions will probably be oriented toward preventing that situation, and you won't care about your friendships for the time being. You must first feel safe and secure before wanting to socialize.

Maslow's hierarchy gives us a template for diagnosing ourselves and what occupies our mental bandwidth more than we might think. You may be stuck at stage one—physiological fulfillment. If so, you might feel like you just need to get everything together and focus on yourself for a while. You're searching for resources and security, and your decisions will (and should) reflect that.

Can you ascertain whether you are having issues with the following? (This is the hierarchy starting from the bottom.)

- Survival
- Security in accommodation and employment
- Personal and familial safety and health
- Relationships and friendships
- Romantic relationships and sexual intimacy
- Self-esteem and confidence
- Acceptance of self
- Self-actualization and fulfillment

If you are struggling with one stage, you know that nothing above or further than that stage matters to you. Whatever your concern is will color your perception, analysis, and decision making on a subconscious level.

Sometimes, people look at the various options in front of them and behave as though their current needs are the only needs they'll ever have. But looking back on your life, you can probably see how wrong this is, and that what constitutes as "good decision" changes with time, and really depends on you and what your needs are in the moment. For example, a person preoccupied at the physiological needs level may make career decisions that heavily favor the acquisition of wealth, while those at higher levels may also factor in the value of family life, of personal fulfilment, or of pursuing higher goals like charity.

Maslow's hierarchy is just one framework of looking at your subconscious needs. The next framework is Tony Robbins's six fundamental human needs.

## Tony Robbins's Six Fundamental Human Needs

This framework comes from famed motivational speaker, Tony Robbins. These six needs drive our lives in ways that we can articulate and others that we would never have thought. Again, understanding what your primary needs are will give clarity as to what's going on in your brain during tough or even daily decisions.

According to Tony Robbins, we generally value two out of the six needs the most at any given time. These two primary needs play a tremendous role in the kind of choices and decisions we make, as well as the habits we develop on a daily basis.

If you can understand these subconscious desires, you can make better decisions and short-circuit your negative impulses and emphasize your positive ones. Reading what follows, you can probably see some overlap with Maslow's needs.

**The Need for Certainty.** The need for certainty is about the assurance that you can avoid pain and gain pleasure, which is best done through routine and stability.

The more certain and secure we feel in the predictability of our well-being, the more comfortable we feel engaging in other activities. This is why we crave predictability and assurance in our lives. These are very important because they ensure one extremely important goal: survival.

The more certain we are that there is no danger, the more we can relax to focus on other needs. Certainty forms the bedrock of our hierarchy of needs. Certainty ensures survival, and once this is taken care of, we can then look toward other needs.

However, the other side of the spectrum is when you feel certainty has been established. Think about it. Would you want to watch a basketball game if you already knew the score and everything that would happen in that game? Probably not. That would be boring and predictable.

Everyone requires different levels of certainty in their lives. For example, my own need for certainty is very low compared to others. I travel constantly and always have new hobbies. If things become too routine, I get bored very easily. I need to constantly challenge myself with the next need, which is in direct conflict with the need for certainty.

This need can lead to analysis paralysis, however, if we are unable to at without feeling like we can predict the outcome with one hundred percent accuracy.

**The Need for Uncertainty and Variety.** The mirror opposite of the need for certainty is the need for the unknown and variety. This is the need for change and new stimuli.

We all need a change of scenery every now and then. The idea of novelty is attractive for a reason, and it's simply to experience something new and be surprised at an outcome rather than know it before you begin.

Do you want to watch the same type of movie over and over? Most people don't, but if you do, you might gather that you have a low need for uncertainty and variety. Too much uncertainty brings us fear, but not enough uncertainty will bring us a lack of fulfillment.

It's why most people enjoy traveling and eating new foods. We don't want to do the exact same thing over and over again. This is what makes life exciting, because we don't know what to expect. We have a need for the adrenaline that only novel stimulation can bring us. Routine is death (for some).

Variety brings pleasure even though it may result in a lesser chance of safety and survival.

**The Need for Significance and Uniqueness.** Deep down we all need to feel that we are important, unique, and special. We don't want to feel insignificant and that no one cares about us.

We want to be the special snowflakes that we like to imagine we are. We all want to stand out in a positive way and be known for something.

This is manifested in many different ways. Some will go out of their way to achieve in an academic sense, deriving their sense of worth in that realm. Everyone creates an identity of themselves based on their self-perception of how they're special.

If you've noticed someone that appears to be dressing solely for attention, they're taking pride in their unique appearance. They feel significant because they stand apart from everybody else.

No one would state their goal is to be indistinguishable from their neighbor, so this is a very natural inclination. However, taking things too far to the extreme can turn off most people. You can imagine this in the form of people who dress obnoxiously or who constantly feel the need to discuss how different they are.

Additionally, if you strive for too much significance and differentiation, you may relate to others less and less, which makes the next human need difficult. In the decision-making realm, the need to be unique is actually a great way to cut through mountains of information and identify what matters most to *you*.

**The Need for Connection.** We all have an instinctual need to bond and connect with others. We strive for interpersonal relationships because they make us feel validated, important, and social. We want to feel like we belong and are part of a tribe.

Some people are extremely family-oriented and travel in packs, where others are lone wolves that enjoy their own company. Some of us like to play team sports, while others like to run alone along the beach. There's a happy medium somewhere for everyone.

The basis for most of these connections is similarity and familiarity. You might call that convenience or opportunity, but the truth is that most relationships start there and evolve from that point.

It's easier to like somebody who is somewhat similar to you, because you can better relate to them. It feels more natural. This is why I mentioned earlier in our need for significance that we can't overdo things to such an extent that we destroy all similarity. We can be different, but not too different; otherwise, you're only going to connect with other outliers.

The need for significance versus connection is like trying to feed Goldilocks stew. If our need for connection is not being met, we feel alone and disjointed from people. However, if it's met entirely, we no longer feel different or unique, and we end up lacking a sense of significance.

**The Need for Growth.** Everybody is looking to expand and increase capacity and capabilities.

Everybody is looking to achieve their goals and move onto the next. Very few people are content simply watching television every day and starting the process over on the next. Most of us need a sense of progress and enjoy working toward something.

Everything on earth either grows or dies— that's not a false dichotomy. Human beings are no exception to this. We must feel we're constantly growing in our lives and moving forward.

The real litmus test occurs when you achieve a goal you set for yourself. Maybe it was a certain financial target, a certain lifestyle, or that new computer. Are you satisfied and no longer feel the need to keep reaching, or do you move the goal posts and start to plan how to exceed your original goal?

Those with a strong need for growth will be unhappy until they set a new goal because they're not growing anymore. To many of us, living life from day to day without an overarching goal and theme becomes an exercise in futility.

**The Need for Contribution.** Finally, we all have the need for a sense of contribution to society.

It might be a service to our community or giving money to a cause, but deep down, we all want to feel that we make an impact and won't pass from this earth without anyone caring. We want to make a mark on the world in our time and be memorable by contributing to society as a whole.

How many people will attend our funerals, and how much will they care?

This explains the popularity of volunteering and philanthropy. It's a universal need that exists in varying degrees in people. We want to give and contribute to a greater good above ourselves simply because it feels good and fulfills our sense of contribution to the world.

When you see a homeless person, do you feel compelled to give or do you ignore them? Do you want your work to affect thousands of people, or are you content just working for yourself?

This entirely different set of subconscious needs and desires, again, vary in each person, even if they appear to manifest the same. For example, your friend might be exercising fanatically because they have a need for certainty in their physical appearance and significance, but you might view exercise as fulfilling the need for personal growth. It is the same outward manifestation, but entirely different needs are satisfied.

On the other hand, you might have the same needs as someone else, but they are manifested in completely different ways. For example, you and your friend both have strong needs for uncertainty and variety. You fulfill it through traveling, but they fulfill it through changes of romantic partners.

How does all of this relate to making better decisions? It can sometimes feel like mulling over decisions is something we do objectively and neutrally, but it's this very assumption that makes our decision making vulnerable to error. Making decisions is a subjective process, so that's why it's important to understand who you are and what you are using to guide these decisions—consciously or unconsciously.

Evaluate which of the six needs resonate with you and try to identify how attempting to satisfy these needs influences your decisions on a daily basis. Self-understanding is paramount to success, because otherwise, you're just winging it.

## Your Values

If you've found yourself asking the question "who am I?", you might have also been asking simultaneously, "What should I do?"

Our lack of genuine identity can show itself in an inability to make decisions, to choose a path, to set a goal, or to say what we want—in other words, what we *do* is a reflection of who we *are*. If we have a problem with one, we usually have a problem with the other.

So, this is where we'll begin. If you're unsure of how to act, you're also probably a little unsure of who you are. Knowing how best to act is a question of knowing what kind of person you are. If you are someone who prioritizes family and social connection above anything else, for example, you don't need to think too hard about the dilemma of working late nights at the office versus spending quality time with your young children. Your identity informs your choices.

In fact, how we respond to life's dilemmas, choices, and difficulties says a lot about the strength of our own values. We are as we do, and we do according to what we value. Inner values and principles are like a personal manifesto that tells us how to act in any situation. This is our own code of ethics that we've devised for ourselves, and it acts like a guiding light even when—or maybe particularly when—the path is unclear.

How shall we define "values"?

A value is a judgment that makes claims about the priorities we hold in life. **They are principles, rules, or beliefs that give meaning to our lives.** They are what stop life from feeling empty and meaningless, because they are inherently *about* meaning—it's whenever you say, "Thing A is more important and valuable than thing B." In saying this, it follows that the right thing to do is thing A.

Values not only guide our action when we're unclear, they give us strength to carry on when the path might be clear but the journey difficult. You might have a really difficult time turning down those extra hours at work, but when you can tune into the deeper value of being present in your children's lives as they grow up, you are given strength to make a decision that makes you unpopular at work.

Granted, many of the values you might hold, consciously or unconsciously, are secondhand. They come to us from our cultures, our parents, our religion, our political environment, even our historical era. Some values might be held uncritically, i.e. you may have them simply out of habit, and haven't really examined them closely. Others might be personally chosen after extensive deliberation. Values can change over time. We might rebel against the values of our group, accept them completely, or negotiate a little, but we always have the option to be more conscious and deliberate about our own values. If you were put on the spot right now and asked what your values were, how quickly and easily do you think you could answer? Do you think you could easily list five or ten of the things you most value in life? Going even further, could you say confidently that your life mostly aligns with these values? It's one thing to *know* what's right, but there's very little point in devising a complete book of rules that you never really intend to follow.

Though the self-help industry might sometimes have you believe otherwise, your identity isn't just something you go shopping for like you do a pair of sneakers or a brand of shampoo. You cannot just pick and choose values—they need to be a *genuine* expression of what you really do care about. This can seem a little like a catch-22 situation—you don't have an identity so you need to find your values, but how do you know which values you care about without having an identity?

The process is not as difficult as it seems.

Firstly, know that the process isn't done all at once—you are not going to uncover a complete and fully-functioning self in an afternoon and start living your best life once you wake up tomorrow morning. It's a *process*, and insight will come in fits and starts. In fact, a life well-loved might be one in which you continually revisit the question of identity, with your answers deepening on every attempt.

We also need to remember that, in finding values, we are the ultimate arbiters. We decide. So, you might need to take the time to tune out every other voice so you can better hear your own. There is no wrong way to do it. There's no right answer. There's only what works for *you*.

Having said that, people are motivated by a lot of different values, which it might help to consider in finding out our own:

*Financial independence or wealth*

*Being in nature*

*Romantic love or connection with others*

*Having freedom and independence*

*Learning and knowledge*

*Fun and adventure*

*Good physical health and fitness*

*Spiritual or religious pursuits*

*Art and creativity*

*Work accomplishments, leadership, business*

*Security and survival*

*Social cohesion and harmony in a group*

*Peace, calm, and contentment; relaxation*

*Honor, loyalty, and dependability*

. . . and so on.

You might look at all of the above and think that they're all valuable. But the trick is in identifying your *priorities*—those things that are best, that bring the most satisfaction and meaning. You may care about creative expression and individuality, but your love of family stability may trump that ten times over. You need to know how each of your needs and preferences rank relative to each another.

A good way to find out what matters most is to ask what has seemingly bought you the most happiness and sense of meaning in the past. If you look at all your high points in life, and they all involved adventure and freedom to travel and explore, that tells you something. It works the other way around too: in thinking of your life's most painful memories, why did they hurt so much? Could it be that these events were moments when your deepest values were disappointed or violated? Tally up the achievements you're genuinely proud of and see what they have in common. Or, look more closely at your worst failures and blunders and ask why they stung particularly badly—were these times where you acted *against* your values?

Another trick is to look at the people you admire or wish to be like (or even envy)—what values do they exemplify? If all your role models and heroes are self-made entrepreneurs, is this telling you about the value you place on financial independence? Maybe. Or maybe what appeals to you about them is that they're unique and following their own dreams, breaking the rules. Or maybe they are reflecting your yearning for a life filled with more admiration and recognition.

Since you are uncovering your values rather than creating them from scratch, another general technique is to look at all the decisions you are currently making—they may speak strongly to values you might not yet be aware you actually have. Watch yourself closely for a few days or a week, and notice your decisions when faced with a choice to make. Notice how you feel when you choose one thing over another.

It might be that you notice yourself often choosing things that leave you feeling bad, and don't really feel aligned with who you are. It may be that you notice key decisions reflecting your values. Either way, we are already living by values every moment of every day—it's simply a question of becoming aware of them and asking whether they're the choices that best reflect the values we hold—or want to hold.

Look for patterns. See if you can find any strong feelings one way or another—are there any non-negotiable sentiments? What are you absolutely unwilling to do or give up? Why? What choices make you feel proud and content, and which ones feel like a compromise, an obligation, or even something you're embarrassed about?

Feeling right, however, is just one aspect that helps determine your values. You also need to make informed decisions about what you really believe in that rely on more than just your emotional inclinations at any given time. Say you're confused about whether you value your career or your connection with friends and family more. You've found that abandoning your family for work often leaves you feeling guilty, and so you think maybe you value your family more than your career. The next step here is to try to find out *why* you feel that way. There can be many factors external to yourself that are influencing this feeling of guilt. Maybe you just have FOMO (fear of missing out), or your family has ingrained a value system in you that says work should always come second.

To get a clearer picture of what valuing something really entails, it helps to read a little on the various reasons why one might want to prioritize something over the other. We are rarely aware of all the reasons one or the other might be a good idea. Just a few searches will yield several reasons for either choice. When reading these, don't just think about which reasons sound more appealing, think about what feels *right* to you. These will often have a lot to do with what your goals in life are. Are you really ready to sacrifice personal success to have a stronger bond with your family? Or would you rather focus on your career while ensuring your family is important, but not paramount? Thinking in this way will prevent you from repeating the earlier cycle of simply having imbibed certain values from your surroundings without really considering what matters most to *you*.

Values (and the identity that comes with them) are not abstract. They are real, lived things, out there in the world. They express themselves in actions and choices. True, they may not always be expressed perfectly all the time. But the *intention* is to live by them. They are a yardstick by which to measure your life, whether you achieve that standard or not. This is why it's more effective to look at your actual life in action when considering values, rather than just sitting down with a piece of paper and pulling nice-sounding ideas out of your imagination. Remember, we are striving for the *real* self, and not just another false self.

Now that we've seen what value-discovery *isn't* (it's not about goals, other people's opinions, or switching out one false self for another one), we can look more closely at what it is. Here's a step-by-step guide to bring you closer.

STEP ONE: CLEAR YOUR MIND

If we wish to fill ourselves up with something new, we first need to pour out all the old that's already there, and start fresh. We need to let go of any bias, expectations, or preconceived notions. Being fixed in our thinking, we can imagine we already know the answer to everything—but this understandably undermines the process of discovery. You really need to trust that there is something for you to learn, something unknown out there that you are willing to encounter openly.

It's difficult, but try to drop (at least temporarily) any preconceived ideas about who you are. Your conscious mind may want to jump in and tell you a narrative

44

("you're an introvert, you're a worrier, you're XYZ"), but set these aside and give some space for your unconscious mind to come to the fore and see new possibilities. We have all been taught which values are "better" than others—we need to forget this lesson if we want to find our *own* values for ourselves!

STEP TWO: START A LIST

Remember that values aren't chosen, they're clarified. Trust that you already have them, you just have to *discover* them. You don't want to inadvertently write down a list of all the things that other people expect you to be.

Scan the list given earlier and see if any of them spark your interest. If not quite, how could you tweak them so they seem more valuable in your opinion? When compiling a list, start broadly and don't censor yourself. Add anything that strikes you as important. You might begin by writing "love," but on further reflection, tease that out a bit more. What kind of love, and why? You might decide that what you really value is brotherly love, friendships, belonging to a

45

community. You could then put "community" on the list and see if that spurs any further values.

As you go, draw on both your best and worst life memories to guide you, as described above. The moments you felt most yourself—what was happening, and what were you doing? The moments when you felt frustrated, violated, disappointed, or uncomfortable—what was not happening, and what does this tell you about the feelings you hold dear?

You might recall the greatest day of your life so far, the birth of your first child. In thinking about why this felt so amazing, you jot a few more notes on your list. You realize that you felt a deep, deep sense of purpose knowing that you now had someone to look after. You examine those feelings of hope, of dedication, of amazement. You realize that being a parent satisfies some of your core values—selfless love, belonging, trust, and hope for the future.

Ask yourself questions to dig closer toward those things in life that bring a sense of meaning. What makes a good day good? What makes you proud and grateful? What makes life worth living (i.e. you'd be miserable without it)? Look not only at the standards you hold for yourself, but those you hold for others. What is a deal breaker for you in your relationships? What is your idea of a person *not* living a meaningful and purposeful life?

STEP THREE: PULL IT ALL TOGETHER

Eventually, you should have a long list of things you value. Though all of these things are important, they can probably be distilled down to a few *main* core values. Read over the notes you've made and see if you can group them into chunks. For example, "community," "friendship," and "compassion for others" have a lot in common, as do "independence," "freedom to follow my own path," and "part-time employment."

Remember, you are not judging anything you have on the list. If you genuinely identify it as a value, put it down. If, on further reflection, you really don't care all that much about innovation or winning awards, then leave them out. As you work (without attachment or judgment!), you should start seeing some clarity emerge. As much as you can, try to connect these ideas to real life—are these values you've actually experienced before meaningful, or have you just been raised or socialized to assume that you want them?

Once you have some clusters of values, see if you can dig deep and identify the main theme uniting them all. In our examples above, friendship, compassion, and community all have one thing in common: the joy of shared human connection. Take your time with this—what is it, really, that makes all of the things on your list so appealing to you?

STEP FOUR: RANK YOUR VALUES

Some people might find that, even after clustering, they're still left with a big list. But, life is filled with choices, and since we are limited, we are often called on to choose between two important and worthwhile things. This is why we need to clarify further and prioritize our values.

You now want to whittle down to those essential values that you absolutely cannot live without. The most fundamental, most basic needs of yours, without which you'd be completely lost, miserable, or pointless. Even if you can identify a few of these, try to choose between five and ten values that you feel neatly capture the dimensions of what's most important to you.

Then, rank them in order of importance. You might do this in ten minutes or find you need a few days to really contemplate it deeply. Use your feelings as a guide, and remember not to rush—you are setting aside everything you know about your false self so that you can meet the acquaintance of your real self—that takes time!

STEP FIVE: LET YOUR VALUES COME ALIVE

If you write something like "physical health and fitness" as a core value, it may seem a little abstract. Time to embed this sentiment out in the real world and put it into context! You want to put these newly discovered core values into a shorthand form that will inspire you every time you look at it, and remind you precisely of the best things in life—according to your most authentic self.

For the person valuing physical fitness, a single beautiful image of a ballet dancer in a powerful leaping pose, mid-flight, might capture the essence of what you value so much: pushing against the limits of human physicality to find beauty and expression in the joy of having a living, moving body. Or, you might find that a certain phrase or quote captures your core value better, a bit like a mission statement. Find a stimulus that triggers a strong emotional reaction— it's these emotions that point you in the right direction and speak more directly to your inner self than any dry, abstract language could.

STEP SIX: TRY THEM ON FOR SIZE

No, you're not done quite yet! Value discovery is an ongoing process. Once you've identified and condensed your core values, see how they fit out in real life. Leave the list for a while and come back to it, seeing how it feels. Do you feel comfortable, in alignment, and clear . . . or are some things still not quite feeling like "you"? Look for the hidden voice of your parents, your culture, etc., and ask whether they've been swaying your list or the way you rank things. If your intuition pipes up, listen to what it says. This may sometimes feel like vague, flimsy work, but rest assured that you are exploring exciting new realms that many people never give themselves permission to enter.

And that's that. Your core values distilled into a concentrated essence that tells you a lot about who you are as a person, and helps you answer a range of questions from, "What should I do?" to, "What do I want right now?"

**Takeaways**:

- Often, decisions can be consciously articulated. If you want Chinese food for dinner, that's easy to justify. But for both quicker and bigger decisions, you are likely more influenced by your subconscious than you realize. The importance of knowing potential subconscious influencing factors is thus extremely high to deciphering your actions.

- There are three models of subconscious needs and desires, the first of which is Maslow's hierarchy of needs. He articulates the following needs: physiological fulfillment (like food and shelter), safety, love and belonging, self-esteem, and self-actualization (a level which he claimed few people reach). Identifying your location in the hierarchy is identifying your subconscious needs, which can then inform how you appraise different choices in life.
- By making these unconscious needs conscious, we give ourselves more clarity and control over the process of making decisions. Maslow's theory also reminds us that our needs can and do change over our lifetime, and we need to factor this in for longer term decisions.
- The next model is Tony Robbins's six needs: love and connection, certainty, uncertainty and variety, significance, contribution, and growth.
- Robbins believed that each of us is motivated to act by at most two of these

needs, which guide how we act and what we value in the world.

- Unlike Maslow's hierarchy, these needs function like traits and are present in different quantities in people, as well as being expressed in endless different ways. Pinpoint your particular needs and understand your decision process better.
- There is nothing inherently better or worse about any of the levels in the hierarchy, or between the six fundamental needs. It's more about discovering what is actually motivating you so that the decisions you make are satisfying your needs.
- Understanding your needs helps you discover your values and principles, ensuring the decisions you make fulfil you on a deeper level.
- A value is a rule, principle, or belief that gives meaning to your life. It is usually something you consider very important in life and base many of your decisions around. This is why when you're confused about what to do in a certain situation or circumstances that you find yourself in, the cause is usually a lack of clarity on what your real values are.

- The first step to discovering what your values are is to simply abandon all preconceived notions you have of who you are. Often, the values we have been living by are actually derived externally. This can be through our family, culture, historical era, etc. By starting from a clean slate, we avoid such influences from clouding our judgment regarding our true values.
- Next, think about the things that you feel most strongly about. This could be personal success, close family bonds, serving others in the form of social work, etc. Finding one will often lead you to other values you hold because they point to a "higher" value you possess. Thus, valuing family over career means that your interpersonal relationships in general are valuable to you.

## Chapter 2. Primed for Good Decisions

The key to truly making good decisions is to understand how your brain processes decisions.

In the prior chapter, we covered the subconscious motivations that underlie your decision making. These are factors that operate without your knowledge and are much more powerful than your conscious motivators.

As the name of the chapter denotes, here we are going to cover a few factors that set the grounds for better and more effective decision making.

In 2014, Swiss researchers discovered the area of the brain involved during decision making. It's mostly the prefrontal cortex, which includes functions such as planning, deciding, calculating, analyzing, problem solving, and decision making. These are generally known as executive functions. The prefrontal cortex is activated during all decision-related thinking, and yet, it is not infinite or unlimited.

Like our bodies, our brains have limits and cannot carry on forever. If we run a marathon, we grow tired and fatigued from over-use. Our muscles cramp, especially the muscles that are used over and over, such as the quadriceps and calf muscles. It's the exact same in the context of making decisions.

## Ego Depletion

Our brains have a limited number of decisions we can meaningfully analyze and make every day, and the more decisions we look at, the more fatigued we get. The prefrontal cortex is like our calf muscle that grows tired and eventually stops working in the correct way. At that point, you're likely to make a decision out of impatience or become frozen in your tracks.

This is a phenomenon more generally known as *ego depletion*.

Ego depletion is the idea that our mental resources for specific activities are limited. The ego can be thought of like an organizing executive who constantly has to appraise information and make decisions. When the resources drain or are decreased, those specific mental activities perform poorly. It was first discovered in relation to self-control, where experiments (Baumeister et al., 1998) showed that subjects who resisted chocolate performed worse and gave up earlier on a puzzle task. In other words, ego depletion was in full effect, and the amount of self-control they exhibited in resisting the chocolate directly weakened their ability to persist with the puzzle task. Decision quality decreased quickly as ego depletion started to take place.

Once you get over the initial surprise that something as small as self-control can actively deplete your mental resources, you begin to find that it makes all too much sense. The brain requires energy to act and think. In fact, the brain requires up to twenty percent of our daily energy consumption, despite being only two percent of the mass of our bodies. It works hard, and the act of self-control is not something that's easy, nor is it infinite.

The thought process involved in the debate over indulging in chocolate or not can be quite lengthy, and as the experiment showed, it can eliminate your capacity for self-control and discipline in the future. It's easy to resist chocolate once or twice, but when you encounter the temptation repeatedly throughout the day, your self-control will likely erode, and it will become nearly impossible to say no—because your brain will run out of juice to do so.

Further support for the theory of ego depletion came in the form of feeding versus starving the brain, and then seeing what happened while using self-control.

Experiments showed that using self-control depleted the brain of glucose, it's primary energy source, and that ingesting sources of nutrition and glucose could reverse the ego depletion and energize people's sense of discipline and self-control. Self-control uses a significant amount of your brain's power reserves, and purely exercising self-control can make you function noticeably lower overall.

How does this relate to making decisions? Besides the fact that any important decision will probably involve a lot of self-control, ego depletion has its own special label in this context: *decision fatigue.*

Decision fatigue is when you make too many decisions and use up all of the mental bandwidth in your prefrontal cortex, leaving any subsequent decisions short-sighted or improperly analyzed. Your ability to make decisions is limited, so you must conserve it and know what trivial decisions to avoid or minimize.

Let's take the simple example of sitting down in a restaurant and opening up the menu. Unfortunately, the menu is about twelve pages, front and back. It unfolds like a map and has enough space to document the rise and fall of the Roman Empire.

This is going to be annoying no matter what, but let's imagine how you might fare in two scenarios.

In scenario one, it is Sunday morning and you are waking up fully rested; in scenario two, it is Tuesday night after a twelve-hour day at a work conference. In the first situation, you might be willing to thumb through the menu for a few minutes to optimize your decision. In the second situation, you would probably give up and select the cheapest hamburger because you can't be bothered at that point in the day.

No matter how rational or thoughtful you might be, it's impossible to make decisions without decreased efficacy. If you make twenty decisions in the morning, you'll probably splurge on an entire pie for lunch, buy a new bathrobe on the way back to the office, and then become angry and irritable when someone asks you what kind of format you prefer your reports in.

You may not be aware that you're tired, and you might be physically fit and alert, but the lack of mental resources will usually push you onto one of two paths.

The first path is acting impulsively and missing or altogether skipping analysis and important factors. This may not matter if you're only trying to decide what to have for lunch. A hamburger or a taco won't have any long-term implications. However, there are plenty of scenarios in which the failure to consider every single factor can be either financially, physically, or mentally harmful.

The second path that stems from decision fatigue is to do nothing at all and postpone a decision for another day. This might make you feel better, but it usually causes more problems in the long run, especially if these are any time-sensitive considerations. It might feel like a relief to push things off, but it's not a reality in a life filled with duties and obligations.

It's clear in both cases that decision fatigue is a suboptimal choice and leads to even worse outcomes.

Something as small as having to think hard in the morning about what you're going to wear or thinking about what you are going to order at your local coffee shop—it's things as small and trivial as these that can seriously short-circuit and deplete our brains for the rest of the day. If it leads you to think, "Oh, forget it. Let's just pick one and get it over with," that's the effects of decision fatigue. They are small acts, but they have greater consequences than you'd think.

## Combat Decision Fatigue

Decision power can be easily drained, so the question is how to safeguard this reservoir of brain power to use when you need it. How can you keep yourself primed for big decisions as often as possible?

First, time your decisions wisely. You can do this in two ways: first, make your big decisions early in the day or week, and second, always make them after a break. If you make decisions early and well timed, you are doing what matters first before daily life robs you of energy. The purpose here is to make sure your brain fed is well fed and rested and generally functioning at a high level so you can properly analyze decision factors.

You can't do this if you are constantly harassed by trivial decisions beforehand or your brain is starved for glucose. Sleep on it, or eat on it. Don't rely on your self-control or willpower as the first line of defense. Instead of putting yourself in situations where you have to use them, conserve them by developing preemptive habits to reduce mental fatigue. So, wake up and face your biggest challenge of the day, rather than waiting till you're tired and crabby and hungry for dinner.

Second, you should try to get a sense of what is trivial in your day so you can either ignore it, consciously make a quick decision about it, delegate it, or automate it.

How do you know if it's trivial? If it's truly trivial, it won't matter if you ignore it, or the choices you make will have no ill effect that lasts longer than a few minutes. This is a tough step for most of us because we are trained to give our full and undivided attention to something, lest we perform it poorly. In a way, this point advocates simply seeing what you can get away with paying little attention to—for your decision fatigue's sake.

Trivial decisions should only be allocated a trivial amount of decision bandwidth, so just try to keep things proportional. If something doesn't impact your life, are you losing anything by not taking action, picking a "good enough" option, or delegating the power of the decision to someone else? Doubtful. Get it off your plate as soon as possible.

The overall aim of this point is to make fewer choices a day. Instead of even dealing with some decisions, you could also choose to automate them—in other words, pick only one option and stick with it for consistency and easy. In a sense, you are making rules for yourself to ignore your choices and stick with, for instance, one lunch, one outfit, one music playlist, and one method of doing things. This is the purported reason famous Apple founder Steve Jobs had a standard uniform of sneakers, a black turtleneck, and comfortable jeans. It was so he could avoid making decisions and save his brainpower for when he actually needed it. On a daily basis, this can truly accumulate.

When you can make parts of your life more predictable, you can focus on the fewer parts that are unpredictable.

Third, if you've got big, multipronged decisions to think about on Tuesday, act like an athlete. This takes the first step to the extreme. That means to prepare and rest for Tuesday and lay off the heavy activity on Sunday and Monday. Your mental resources always recharge, but they are easily depleted. Get into battle mode and treat your brain like a muscle that you need for peak performance.

Fourth, when you're in the decision-making process, attempt to allot yourself more time than you think is necessary. The reason for this is twofold. First, you will always take longer than you think, and second, feeling rushed is bad for decision making because it creates stress and anxiety. The latter point is far more important because it uncovers the role of anxiety and stress in decision-making efficacy.

They are *terrible* for it. Most recently, a 2016 study published in the *Journal of Neuroscience* found that anxiety disrupts prefrontal cortex neuronal functioning. Remember what this area is mainly involved in? That's right—decision making and analysis of costs and benefits. Decisions made under stress are incredibly impulsive and ineffective, notwithstanding the fact that stress is simply one of life's greatest distractions.

Let's take the following scenarios. In Scenario A, you are in a foxhole during World War II and you are being shot at. Explosions are all around you, and the person to your left suddenly collapses to the ground. The rain is starting to pour, and your weapon stops working. Your foxhole starts flooding, and you can hear a tank roll closer and closer.

In Scenario B, you have just woken up by the natural sunlight, and on a table in the room is left a splendid breakfast. It has croissants, jams, jellies, juices, and a stack of eight pancakes. The window is open and you feel a gentle breeze that smells like fresh flowers and dew on the trees.

Which of those scenarios do you think you would be able to make a better decision in? Probably the one with less stress, fewer distractions, and more mental resources available.

There's also a plethora of evidence, most recently confirmed in 2014 in a study at Columbia University Medical Center, to suggest that impulsive and knee-jerk reactions usually turn out to be very bad or wrong. In the study, it was found that a delay of even half a second to one second more before making a decision exponentially improved the outcomes.

Taken together, it's very clear that stress, anxiety, and any type of pressure to make a decision are detrimental to making clear-minded, effective decisions.

## Lower Transaction Costs

The final method of battling decision fatigue is to lower *transaction costs*. Transaction costs, or friction costs, is an economic term for the cost you must expend to be in the market. Whenever you do something, you have some sort of cost associated with it. The cost may be monetary, such as an investment to start a business. For us, it's tied to the *ego depletion* cost in our brain's continued functioning. These are simply the costs, or obstacles, you have to swallow to participate in making a decision.

When you make a decision, good or bad, you incur a cost. The aim then is to manipulate your transaction costs for decisions. Specifically, you want to minimize your transaction costs for good decisions while increasing the transaction costs for bad decisions. You want to encourage good decisions, such as eating healthy or managing your time, by making them easier for you so that they "cost" less. Meanwhile, flip the tables and make bad habits, like being disorganized, having poor time management, and procrastinating, too expensive to entertain.

How do you manipulate transaction costs in this way?

In simpler terms, if you want to encourage good decisions, you must make it easy— almost the default option if possible. For instance, if you want to practice an instrument more, what are the costs involved there that you can control? You can make it easier to practice your instrument by leaving it on your desk, making clear notes as to what to practice, giving yourself fun goals, and clearing time in your schedule every day to practice. You are making it easy to make the decision that is optimal.

It requires a bit of upfront work, but when you set yourself up thusly, you will have lowered the transaction costs and made it easy to make a good decision whether your ego is depleted or not.

You can make poor decisions cost too much in a similar way. For instance, if you wanted to raise the transaction costs of eating poorly, you would remove all junk food from your house, only buy healthy snacks, put bottles of water everywhere around your workspace so you don't feel the angst of hunger, and learn healthy substitutes for fatty food options. You are making it easy to ignore the decision that is suboptimal.

If it helps, you can think of transaction costs as the amount of willpower you must exercise. Thus, the lower the transaction costs are in general, the more willpower you can conserve for the decisions that truly matter. Think of it as a way to make doing the wrong thing "expensive" and the right thing easy, "cheap" and automatic.

A major key to effective decision making is to understand how decision fatigue will impact you. It's more than a folksy concept or an excuse for being lazy. Decision fatigue and ego depletion are very real, but you may have simply become used to it If the phrase, "Okay, just pick one. I don't care anymore," is familiar, you've been through it. If you find yourself feeling irritated, indecisive or even apathetic around decisions, that's a big clue that things could be better I this area. We'll look at analysis paralysis in more detail in a later chapter, but for now, the conclusion is that if we only have limited brainpower, we need to proactively budget that wisely so we are making the best of our decision-making powers.

**Takeaways**:

- The concept of ego depletion is important because it leads directly to decision fatigue. With overuse, certain cognitive processes can flag and wane, in exactly the same way that muscles tire with extended exercise.

- When you reach decision fatigue, your decisions become incredibly suboptimal because you will either become paralyzed or make a rash, unresearched decision. Your willpower will perform weakly, in the same way that tired muscle is just not as strong when it's been working hard already.

- How can you preemptively deal with the effects of ego depletion and willpower fatigue? You can time your decisions wisely such that they made only when rested such as in the morning or after a rest or a meal

- You can categorize the trivial daily decisions you have and make sure to only allot a trivial amount of time to them, drawing limits on how much attention you'll spend on inconsequential decisions. Ask what risks are attached to a decision, the impact it will have, and whether you'll care about it in a month's time.

- You can treat yourself like an athlete and make sure you are mentally tapering off in preparation of big decisions, you can give yourself more time than is necessary to reduce the role of stress and anxiety. Anxiety and low mood can color our decisions. Don't rush!

- You can also work on manipulating your transaction costs to make good decisions more of a default option, while bad decisions are more difficult.
- By automating as many decisions as possible, you take certain decisions out of your hands and get them done without you needing to spend any extra effort. Use tools, habits and routines to make good decisions automatic, saving your mental resources for those truly demanding decisions.

## Chapter 3. The Six Hats, WRAP, ICE, and 3 P

Decision making isn't necessarily a science, but you've seen at least a few methods that strive to put more thought and analysis into decisions.

We started the book by talking about what drives you on a deeper level. We are all driven by subconscious needs, and it's going to be better for you if you can make the subconscious just a little bit more conscious. That requires introspection aside from the act of actually making decisions. In the last chapter, we found ways to remove unconscious obstacles to better decision making, but in this chapter, we'll look at strengthening conscious processes.

This chapter is a more traditional way of thinking about decisions—in that we are seeking to analyze the factors present in insightful ways. These are mostly conscious factors, but they likely include angles and perspectives you've never considered. In a sense, they are templates for you to apply to your own unique situation. They take the information available and shine a different light onto it to aid your quest for optimal decisions.

The first of these such methods is the six hats method.

**The Six Hats Method**

It's one of my favorite decision-making methodologies because it is extremely thorough and focuses on what humans don't excel at—taking different perspectives. The six hats method presents you with a veritable checklist to run through while you try to make a decision, which ensures that all your bases are covered.

We've all heard the term that you must wear more than one hat. The six hats method was created by Edward de Bono, and as you might have guessed, it requires looking at a problem or decision from six separate perspectives by wearing six different hats.

Common advice for making good decisions is to consult mentors, experts or close friends and leverage their unique perspective on your problem—like getting a second pair of eyes to look at things. But this technique tries to do the same, and in fact may be more useful since you learn to switch perspectives yourself. Along with the hats themselves, an avatar that embodies the main purpose of each hat will make matters much clearer. It's like you are making a decision by committee, but all the roles are played by you.

The colors of the six hats are white, red, black, yellow, green, and blue. The colors are fairly inconsequential, and it's probably easier if you categorize them by the avatar. I'll go into each of them in depth.

*"Tell me more. What does this mean, and where did you get that information?"*

The white hat is Sherlock Holmes. This is the thinking and analytical hat. You are trying to gather as much information as possible by whatever means possible. Be observant and act like an information sponge. While you're at it, analyze your information and determine the gaps you have and what you can deduce from what you currently have. Dig deep, fill in the information gaps, and try to gather an understanding of what you really have in front of you.

You want to absorb as much of the available information as you can while also determining what you are missing to make a more informed and more perfect decision. The white hat is also where you should be resourceful about learning. As we discussed earlier, lack of information is one of the worst detriments to your decisions.

Make sure you are armed with information and you seek multiple perspectives and not let yourself be influenced by bias. You want an objective view at the entire landscape. Get out your magnifying glass and start sleuthing, Detective Holmes.

Simple phrases and questions you can use include, "is that really true? What is your evidence?" when looking at premises of an argument you're making, or "what information *don't* I have at this moment, and how can I find it?" when you're weighing up pros and cons or choosing between two options. Basically, you want to get into the perspective of not quite taking your word for it!

*"And how does that make you feel? Why is that?"*

The red hat is Sigmund Freud, the psychotherapist. This is your emotion hat. You are trying to determine how you feel about something and what your gut tells you. Those are not always the same emotion. Combined with the information you collected as Sherlock Holmes, this will already give you a more complete picture than you are used to.

You are asking how you feel about your options and why. Beyond the objective level, decisions affect us on an emotional level. You must account for that—happiness and unhappiness. Emotions are, after all, an indicator of how we are assigning meaning, and how much something is satisfying or violating our deeply held beliefs and values. Emotions add color to our decisions, and feelings are a kind of data that need to be factored into a decision just like any other information.

Ask yourself what you find yourself leaning toward or avoiding and why that might be. You can also attempt to predict how others might react emotionally. Your actions might have consequences beyond your current understanding, and how people will feel is often different from how you think they will feel. What are the origins of your emotions toward each option, and are they reasonable or even relevant, for that matter? Often, our emotions aren't in the open, so when you can understand them better, you will understand your options better.

For example, you might decide that a new project is too difficult and not worth your time, but when you examine your feelings about it, you find that it's really just fear and low self-esteem stopping you. Knowing this about yourself, you can make a clearer decision, and look at the project for its own merits. You might find an emotional inventory reveals powerful and accurate instincts, or it simply shows you some hidden bias you were carrying around— either way, it's good to know about!

*"I don't know. I have my doubts. What about X? Will Y really happen that way?"*

The black hat is Eeyore, the morose donkey from *Winnie the Pooh*. If you don't know who that is, you can imagine the black hat to be the ultimate depressed pessimistic that never believes anything will work out. Indeed, the purpose of the black hat is to attempt to poke holes in everything and to try to account for everything that can go wrong. They are skeptics who always look on the darker side of life.

They believe in *Murphy's Law*: everything that can go wrong *will* go wrong. This is a hat most people never wear because they are afraid to look at their decisions, or reasoning, from a critical point of view. On some level, it probably indicates recognition that their views fall apart under deeper scrutiny, but that is exactly why it's so important to wear the black hat.

It's essentially planning for failure and the worst-case scenario. Planning for success is easy and instantaneous, but what happens when things don't work out and you have to put out fires? How would you plan differently if you thought there was a high probability of failure? Many of us want to be optimistic and hopeful, so we willfully ignore the probabilities of things *not* going our way. In other words, we tend to have a slight bias in imagining that the thing we want is the thing most likely to happen. Then, naturally, we're caught off guard when it doesn't!

You change your approach, look for alternatives, and create contingency plans to account for everything. This is the type of analysis that leads to better planning and decisions because you can objectively take into account what is good and what is not. Wearing your black hat makes your plans tougher and stronger over the long haul, though it can be exhausting to continually reject positivity and hopefulness.

*"It's going to be so great when this all comes together. Just imagine how you'll feel."*

The yellow hat is the cheerleader. It is the opposite of the black hat—you are now thinking positivity and optimistically. This is a motivating hat that allows you to feel good about your decision and the value of putting all the work into it. This is where you turn dark clouds into a silver lining.

It also allows you to project into the future and imagine the opportunities that come along with it. If this decision goes well, what else will follow? Where do optimistic projections place you, and what is necessary for you to reach them?

Belief in yourself is still one of the concepts that fuels achievement and motivation, so it's important to be balanced with pessimism and nitpicking flaws. Yes, you need to have *both* perspectives on your internal decision-making board of directors. Let them talk to each other and hash out probabilities and plans. This is the best way to get a balanced, robust view.

*"Call me crazy, but what if we completely change X and try Y?"*

The green hat is Pablo Picasso, the famous artist. This hat is for creativity. When you wear this hat, you want to think outside the box and come up with creative perspectives, angles, and solutions to whatever you are facing. It can be as simple as pretending that your current leading option is unavailable and having to figure out what you can do instead. You have to deviate from the current options and discover other ways of solving your problem.

Brainstorming is the name of the game here. No judgment or criticism is allowed when you are wearing this hat because you want to generate as many ideas as possible. You can always curate them later, but the more solutions you can think of, no matter how zany or ineffective, there will always be something you can learn or apply from them.

This is also a hat of open-mindedness and not being stuck in one track of thinking, which can be dangerous if you refuse to alter your course in the face of hardships.

*"Now, now, children. Everyone will have their turn to be heard."*

The blue hat is Henry Ford, founder of Ford Motor Company and inventor of the modern assembly line. The blue hat is all about coordinating and creating a system to integrate all the information you obtained from the other hats. You can also look at this hat as the CEO hat: you are in charge of making things happen and putting things in place, though not necessarily in charge of creating anything by yourself.

You are in charge of weighing how heavily each hat should be considered and what factors you must take into account when integrating the information. The CEO knows the context the best, so the input from each different hat is synthesized and weighed based on personal priorities and the situation at hand. You are the ultimate decider.

Now that you know how each hat works, it's time to illustrate how they all work together. Let's suppose you are considering buying a new house.

Wearing the white Sherlock hat, you would examine all the information you have about the current market. That wouldn't be enough, so you would conduct far more independent research on the economy and market trends and come up with a clear sense of how much it will cost you, where you will live in the meantime, and if you are okay with the long-term tradeoff.

You would want prices on everything, data on past prices, predictions on future prices, and the other benefits and drawbacks to living in the new house. Then you'd take all that data and compare it to your current living situation, as well as to other houses in the area.

Wearing the red Freud hat, you would introspect and determine how you feel about the new house emotionally and intuitively. Will it make you happy regardless of the cost? What does your gut tell you? Money certainly can't buy happiness, but it can set the stage for it. Is the new house going to help with that? Are you drained by this process or energized by it? Recall that the red hat suggests you think

about the emotional impact your decision
will have.

Wearing the pessimistic Eeyore black hat,
you would try to plan for the worst-case
scenario for before and after you buy this
new house—for example, if the market
tanks and the house drops in value by half
or if you lose your job and have to relocate
to a new city far away from your new house.
In a darker turn, you might lose your job
and not be able to find a new one, meaning
you'd be saddled with a mortgage that you
can't pay.

What other factors inside or outside of your
control might make purchasing a new
house a terrible decision? The construction
might be faulty, the previous owner might
have lied to you, and the neighbors might
be horrible. Plan for them so you can
account for them.

Wearing the optimistic cheerleader yellow
hat, what is the best-case scenario for
purchasing a new house and how will that
affect and benefit your life? Perhaps the
house will increase twofold in value in the
next three years, and perhaps you will be

able to sell it for a huge profit while still living in the area. It might be a house for your family, so you'll feel stable and secure while in a good school district. Do these outweigh any potential negatives?

Despite all the problems for the new house, it might be nicer than anything you've ever lived in, and it represents a dream come true for you. Worst-case scenario, you can always rent a room to your cousin.

Wearing the Picasso green hat of creativity, you can think of additional ways to solve your problem of wanting to live in a new place. For example, would you sleep on a friend's couch to see if you need a big house? Rent a monthly house in the area first before committing to purchasing? Put in a new stove in your current house and find you won't have to move? What other areas of the city do you want to explore and live in? How else can you invest the money in a safe and smart way? Do you actually want to live in a new home, or do you have other desires?

When you get to the blue Henry Ford hat, your job is to sort through all the information you've uncovered, try to decide what is really important, and use it to make the most informed decision of your life. Perhaps you've decided that the money is simply too tight for a new house, and what you really wanted was to have a nicer kitchen. Or perhaps you've found that the housing market is at an all-time low, so even if you are low on money, it would be one of the best financial decisions to immediately take the leap.

The point of the six hats method is to take a deep dive into a particular perspective and temporarily tune everything else out. Give it free reign and reject all opposition to it for the time being. That's just about the only way you will be able to make a compelling argument for something that you don't wholeheartedly believe in at first. You want to embody the hat you currently wear and have a debate with yourself, moderated by the blue hat.

The hats represent your interests. You'll be able to see clearly which interests of yours you have focused on in the past. They might be interests that you don't prioritize as much as others, but they are your interests regardless. It's all a process to make sure that your top interests win out in the end (if they deserve to).

## It's a WRAP

The other decision methodology comes from a formidable pair of brothers, Chip and Dan Heath, who are professors at Stanford University and Duke University, respectively. It is known as the WRAP methodology, which is an acronym that we'll dive into shortly.

The purpose of the WRAP approach is to make better decisions by focusing on often overlooked factors that tend to have far bigger implications that what we might traditionally look at. It's also what we've sought to do with the checklists and descriptions of subconscious influencers throughout the book.

WRAP works on the assumption that we are always trying to make decisions and generally think with the least amount of work possible. Unfortunately, this is more due to necessity and circumstance—why do more in-depth thinking and analysis when we don't have to and have other things to get to?

Well, we usually have to, which means we take mental shortcuts that often put us onto the wrong path. What do these shortcuts look like? They are countless.

- Imperfect or incomplete information
- Seeing a pattern or causation where there is none
- Influence by a strong emotion
- Overconfidence
- Fatigue
- Laziness
- Incorrect underlying assumptions or beliefs

Even if you're in a rush, WRAP makes you look past those shortcuts and do the work, so to speak, in four thorough steps. WRAP stands for the following:

1. Widen your options.
2. Reality-test your assumptions.
3. Attain distance.
4. Prepare to be wrong.

This stands in stark contrast to most people's decision-making methodology, which might consist of the following (at most):

1. Look at most available options.
2. Select an option.
3. Cross your fingers and hope for the best.

**Widen Your Options.** This is the first step because most people only settle for options that are immediately available and right in front of their faces. They only consider the low-hanging fruit and think in conventional terms, dismissing other approaches for arbitrary reasons.

When you widen and expand the set of options you have, you immediately increase the chances of an optimal decision. This is easier said than done, because we usually think in black and white terms: yes or no, X or Y. We don't consider the possibility that the answer or decision can be *maybe* or Z.

Sometimes just below the surface lies another level of options that you would never have seen if you didn't dive in, kick up the dust, and take a serious look. Even adding one alternative choice will benefit you greatly and provide additional insight into your decision.

Of course, this comes with the negative effect of prolonging a process and increasing inefficiency, but if you are looking for the absolute best option, it's imperative to widen your options.

For example, what options do you have when you want to increase a company's revenue? You can look at the hard assets like training better salesmen, reducing overhead, and downsizing. These are the low-hanging fruit—what other options do you have to increase revenue? What if you looked at how happy your salesmen were, how you could motivate them better, where you are losing money in your vendor contracts, or what sources of needless spending the company engages in? The list is endless.

These are the types of options you need to generate before making a decision. You might not find the very best one, but you are likely to find options that will still greatly impact your bottom line, whatever it may be.

**Reality-Test Your Assumptions.** What does this mean? It means to put your options to the test and go through the motions of what obstacles your options will encounter. Really think through what the future would look like and try to imagine every little detail. Often our options are plagued by confirmation bias and hubris, which means you won't be able to consider them objectively if you become attached to them. That's natural, and that's why it's necessary to go through this step.

It puts your decision on stage in front of an audience full of skeptics, and the skeptics will be lobbing difficult questions and asking you to answer them. They will force you to go through every step and explain in painstaking detail about what will happen next. When airplane manufacturers make sure their airplanes are ready for flight, they put the planes through a rigorous process known as stress testing, which includes flexing the wings and running the plane through physical and electric hardships to make sure that it holds up.

Reality-testing is no different.

Allow others to try to find holes in your option, and realize if you are trying to defend yourself based on rationalizations or based on actual facts and evidence. Of course, you may not have the option of the peanut gallery to ask you questions, so you have to train yourself to ask better questions and mentally visualize each step more consistently.

Let's stay with the example we used earlier of increasing a company's revenue. How might you reality-test your options here? Focus on one at a time and playing them out to their logical conclusion. Go through each step in the process and don't gloss over potential problems by saying, "Oh, we'll take care of that when it comes, no problem."

If you decide to focus on training your salesmen to be more effective and persuasive, you need to look at the costs involved in that and how it will play out in the next year or two, as training is a longer-term process. Then you must act like its biggest critic and ask how much increased revenue you will see, whether it's worth it, if the salesmen are capable of it, how it compares to the other options, when you can expect revenue to increase, how it can be done less expensively, and so on. Start with the five journalistic questions of who, what, when, where, and why, and move on from there.

Remember, you win if you find a flaw. If you don't find any, you still win.

**Attain Distance.** Attaining distance from your option means that you must take a moment and remove yourself from the process. Otherwise, you run the risk of letting your sense of triumph and short-term emotional attachment to an option color your decision.

Emotion can seep into any phase of the WRAP process and completely overpower your sense of logic and analysis. When you find confirmation and validation for your option, its natural to fall into a spiral of confidence and happiness. This is dangerous without distance.

In other words, take some time to sit on your decision. Sleep on it if necessary. Return after some psychological and mental distance to see if your justifications and reasoning still make sense. They might not.

If you've written anything in your life, you might be familiar with this phenomenon. You write something on Monday and it feels like the next Charles Dickens novel. You put it aside and bask in your triumph. When you reread it again the next Monday, you may find that it is barely intelligible. That's the power of distance.

**Prepare to Be Wrong.** Preparing to be wrong isn't assuming that you will be wrong. It's actually a thought exercise in finding alternate options and evaluating how effective they are.

If you succeed with your option, that's great, but success isn't really the scenario we need to plan for. Things are easy when we find success. We need to plan for when things go wrong or not as planned, because that's when we need to come up with a new approach and discover if your options are as good as you think.

In other words, prepare to be wrong by creating a Plan B and possibly Plan C, if possible. No matter how certain you are, unpredictability is still a possibility. Plan so that you can hit the ground running instead of panicking whenever you see a small wrench in your plans. You might even begin your decisions by opting for the best Plan B.

To increase a company's revenue, you might have decided that training your salespeople better is the unquestioned best choice. You've done the reality test and thought through the possibilities. However, what if it doesn't work on account on something you can't possibly control or foresee?

You would want to know what Plan B and Plan C are and how you can move into those seamlessly. What are the first steps so that you don't waste any time scrambling if Plan A falls short? What is going to get you closer to your goal while giving up the smallest cost? Preparing to be wrong is all about how you can adapt to adversity.

The WRAP process and the six hats method

may seem like a lot of work, but all they are doing is uncovering your blind spots. If you are making decisions flying by the seat of your pants and relying upon your laser-sharp instinct, that's only going to lead to good decisions out of luck. And that's not a habit you want to continue.

## The 3 P Technique

Here's a decision-making technique I like for its simplicity. The way your life turns out comes down to two quite opposite forces: the first is luck, and the second is the quality of the decisions you make. In real life, it's usually a mix of *both* these things working together. Now, I'm no philosopher and to be honest it's not important what the exact ratio is of luck to choice. The premise is that as long as we make better decisions, we have some scope to improve our lives.

There's a problem, though. Many of us think of decision making in purely black and white terms. They're either good decisions or bad ones, right or wrong. And we also have a very over simplified way of determining which side a decision falls on: if our decision works out well, we assume that it was the right decision. If things go badly we conclude that whatever we did immediately before was the wrong thing.

Sounds like a logical way to think about things until you remember that other aspect: luck. Imagine a poker game. The one who wins typically needs both aspects on their side. They need good luck to be dealt good cards, and they also need to play well, i.e. to make god decisions with those cards. But that doesn't mean that if someone loses, we can conclude that all their decisions were bad ones, or that if someone wins, all their decisions were good ones. You can make good choices and lose, and bad ones and yet still win. Subtle difference.

In this book so far we've focused on the conscious decision-making aspect, while forgetting that sometimes, luck steps in and affects the outcome. We should remember this when weighing up outcomes and deciding whether out decisions were good or bad (hint—they're usually somewhere in between!). In in poker, we cannot control luck, but we can make predictions and guesses when we make decisions. We can do the same for any decision.

Annie Duke is a world-famous poker player who won millions in poker tournaments, and now has a lot to say about this very phenomenon. She claims that decisions are really predictions for future outcomes—this is easy to see in poker, but perhaps less obvious for the rest of life. Annie Duke explains her decision-making process as 3 Ps. Let's take a closer look.

The first is **preferences**. As a framework and context for all your decisions, you need to actually understand what you're hoping to achieve. You need to have affirm grasp of your own values and what you'd actually like as the ideal outcome. General goals are fine ("I want to find a high paying job that I like."), but it's worth being as specific as possible ("I want XYZ job in such-and-such industry in this area paying twice my current salary.").

It's difficult to truly, objectively say what a good decision really is, but it's far easier (and more likely to be accurate) for you to identify what *you* personally want to happen. You can't just any particular outcome as a bad one or good one—for some it will be good, for others it will be bad. It makes more sense to consider how well that outcome satisfies your particular needs and preferences. Don't just assume theses will be obvious to you, either—often we have to make a conscious effort to tease out what we want and don't want!

The next P is **payoffs**. Once you know what you want, assess the potential benefits, i.e. payoffs. Consider one particular outcomes, and see how it impacts your preferences— does it help or hinder your goals? In real life, decisions usually have *both* good and bad outcomes. You can often only get clarity when you deliberately weigh up both not just relative to one another, but relative to your values and goals.

For example, let's say you're trying to choose between a few new houses to move into. One is cheaper and closer to town but needs a lot of expensive repairs, the other is nicer and bigger, but a bit isolated. These might seem like evenly matched choices, until you factor in your goals and preferences—is being near a city more important to you than being out in nature?

Don't make your decisions merely hypothetical. Literally play out potential outcomes in your mind. Picture yourself in each home, not just next week, but one, five, ten years into the future. See whether the loneliness in house B gets worse or if you're likely to not care too much that House A is smaller. Thought about this way, you get to see not just the wisdom of a particular choice, but a particular choice in *your* world, according to your values.

The final P is **probabilities**. Look at the outcomes you've been conjuring up (the different lives in the different potential homes) and then be as honest as you can about the likelihood of each one occurring. Remember, luck plays a role. And the trick is that you don't know *how much* of a role. There are no guarantees in life, and you may be completely caught by surprise, no matter how good your planning and decision making. For example, knowing that you're single and an extrovert, you predict that moving to an isolated area will drive you crazy within a few years (unless of course you magically meet the love of your life living next door—that'll be the unpredictable chance element!).

Remembering to factor in luck and probabilities does two things: it keeps you on your toes so you never forget that the outcome is not exclusively determined by your actions, and it also frees you to identify and focus on those things where you have the highest chance of making a difference. Don't sweat the truly random things; focus instead on those areas where you have strong reason to believe you are in control. Those are the things that will bring the most likely positive outcomes.

To make a better decision (not a "good" one, but a better one) comes down to making highly educated guesses with the information you have, allowing plenty of room for luck. Combine preferences, payoffs and probabilities and you make better predictions about how life will play out if you follow path A or path B—and choose accordingly.

The 3 P Technique can seem quite obvious on its surface, but if you work through it deliberately, you might be surprised by just how often you fail to factor these considerations in. Nobody ever said humans were rational, huh?

## The ICE Scoring Model

Let's finish this chapter with a final technique, the ICE Scoring Model. This approach comes to use from the world of project management and business strategy, but its principles are just as applicable in everyday decision making. The Ice acronym stands for impact, confidence, and ease. Let's see what each means.

On each of the three parameters, you rate a potential idea, choice, decision, or plan from one to ten, then multiply all these scores together to get a final result. This allows you to rank options, assess different plans of action, or simply get a better idea of the options in front of you. By running this quick calculation, you see immediately where you should be focusing your attention and resources, i.e. which path is worth following.

The technique is great for people in startup environments or innovative workplaces, where decisions have to be made quickly, using as much of the information available as possible.

**Impact** is the potential for you a choice (idea, action, decision, etc.) to serve your main life goals.
**Confidence** is how sure you are that this outcome will actually follow if you make that choice.
**Ease** is, of course, how easy it is to make the decision or take the action.

So, you should prioritize or choose those things that are most impactful, that you are very confident in, and which are relatively easy to do, over those things that are difficult, have uncertain outcomes, and which don't have a massive impact even if they are as effective as possible.

Let's say you're deciding whether you want to go back to college to get a specialist degree to improve your earning potential in the future. But you don't want to waste money and time only to end up earning the same anyway. You look at some choices according to the ICE model as follows:

*Choice 1: Go to college to do a full three-year degree.*
**Impact** – 8/10. Many people with this qualification seem to do very well with it.
**Confidence** – 6/10. On the other hand, who knows what the job market will be in three years' time?
**Ease** – 3/10. It'll be hard work for three solid years.
**Total score**: 17

*Choice 2: Do a smaller one-year certificate that you can complete while still working.*
**Impact** – 5/10. Less of a big deal than the degree, but still useful.
**Confidence** – 9/10. You're pretty sure it *would* make a difference, even if a smaller one.
**Ease** – 6/10. It will be easier than the three-year degree, and quicker to complete.
**Total score**: 20

*Choice 3: Do nothing and keep working at the same job, gaining experience.*
**Impact** – 3/10. The least likely to drastically improve your earning potential on its own, though small promotions are possible.

**Confidence** – 9/10. You're fairly confident that if you change nothing, you'll stay on roughly the same path!
**Ease** – 8/10. Carrying on doing what you are is far easier than learning a new skill set.
**Total score**: 20

Using this system, choice 2 and 3 are best. Maybe there is some extra variable you could consider that tips the scales in one direction, for example you get funding to do the certificate instead of paying for it yourself. As you can see, the ICE technique can sometimes lead to unexpected results—perhaps everyone in your life told you that studying further was a great idea and that you should go for it, but this analysis might at least give you pause. Another thing to notice is that doing nothing is also a choice—and sometimes it's not a bad option!

The ICE model is not all-or-nothing. It's about *prioritizing*. After this analysis, you might decide to seek some in-between solution, like study the big university degree but piecemeal, part time, while continuing to work. This would increase the ease score. You might decide that university is not a great idea *now*, but do the exercise again later and see if your goals, values, and priorities have changed.

The ICE model was created by GrowthHackers CEO Sean Ellis, so its worth remembering that it was created in a particular context. As you can see, the analysis is only ever as good as the options you present yourself with. It's an extremely objective process, so if you are mistaken about your own goals, the ease of which a decision can be made, or are over- or under-confident compared to the real probabilities, your decision making will be biased. Each area is weighted equally, which may be a good or bad thing, depending on your own values and preferences.

On the other hand, the technique is great for simplifying difficult decisions fairly quickly. You don't have to rely on it exclusively, but use it in conjunction with other techniques to quickly give you another insightful perspective on a decision you're facing. The technique is good for decisions you need to make quickly, but which aren't life-or-death. The model was designed for fast-paced business environments, but it's probably not a great way to make truly life changing decisions!

Rather, use this in your work life, or when organizing and managing projects. Use ICE to decide where to focus on when you're short on time and resources. If you have a full day, ICE can help you zoom in on what's most important, most impactful, and most doable for you, moment by moment. Of course, it doesn't hurt to fine-tune your accuracy when it comes to assessing the ease, confidence and impact of certain actions—that is a skill in itself!

**Takeaways**:

- Most of us engage in very little with regards to our decisions. A pros and cons list, perhaps. But this still leaves us victims of your blind spots.
- The six hats method of decision making implores you to view a fork in the road from six distinct different perspectives. Typically these are represented by colors, but avatars are more illustrative. The six

different perspectives to consider are Sherlock Holmes (gather information), Sigmund Freud (emotions), Eeyore the donkey (pessimist), a cheerleader (optimist), Pablo Picasso (creativity), and Henry Ford (information synthesis).

- The WRAP method was devised to specifically address blind spots. WRAP stands for widen your options, reality-test, attain distance, and prepare to be wrong. As you can see, these are not typical ways to approach a decision, though they can serve you well because they represent what is likelier to happen in the real world.

- The 3P technique was created by poker player Annie Duke. It consists of preferences, payoffs and probabilities. Preferences refer to your goals and what you're actually hoping to achieve, payoffs are the potential benefits of different outcomes, and probabilities speaks to the confidence you have in certain predictions of the future. It's these informed predictions that allow us to make good decisions.

- The ICE scoring model also rests on considering three key components of any decision. The first is impact (the potential for you a choice, idea, action, or decision to serve your main life goals), the second is confidence (how sure you are that this outcome will follow your action, bearing in mind that luck and chance play a role), and ease (how easy it is to make the particular decision). A subjectively good decision is one in which has a high probability of having a high impact on your goals, whilst being easy to achieve. The bad decision is the opposite.

- There is overlap between ICE and 3P, and both have limitations, i.e. they depend on our accurate assessment of the three aspects!

## Chapter 4. Mental Checklist

Continuing with the theme of different considerations in making decisions, this chapter presents more factors that have likely never crossed your mind and can make you happier through better selection.

Even though the objectives and factors in any decision are going to be different on any given day, there are still lines of thought you should apply to every one of them for an optimal decision that benefits you and doesn't actively hurt you.

If we are honest with ourselves, the reason we don't engage in this type of thinking is because we are lazy or we don't think we have to. We overrate our ability to make decisions in an odd sense of hubris. We think we should go with our gut or live on our instinct, but study after study has proven our sense of impulsive decisions to be fairly unreliable. But so many skills in life take deliberate practice—why shouldn't decision making be one of them?

The following techniques will slow down your decisions, and give you a chance to think through things carefully before you get carried away with a preferred outcome and forget to consider other aspects. But it will also give you additional templates you can use to make sure all of your bases are covered and you are making the best move for yourself in light of all the relevant factors.

## The 10/10/10 Rule

The first part to incorporate into your mental checklist is the 10/10/10 rule.

The 10/10/10 rule is very straightforward and asks you to travel through time. When you are at a fork in the road, ask yourself how you will feel about the choice you make: ten **minutes** from now, ten **days** from now, and ten **months** from now? Depending on the scope and context of the decision, you can make it longer or shorter terms in nature. Shorter periods of time correspond to decisions with smaller stakes and more immediate consequences, while longer periods of time correspond with larger stakes and more delayed consequences.

If you want to debate eating a slice of pizza, you might do ten minutes, ten hours, and ten days. You'd find that eating a pizza or hamburger in the moment really doesn't affect your life very much in any timeline. If you want to decide what city to move to, you can use ten weeks, ten months, and then ten years in the future. You can see how your decisions can greatly impact your life if you view it through the lens of the future.

Travel through time and explore the consequences in each scenario. The 10/10/10 rule begs you to ask your future self about the decisions and approaches you make today. Make sure you are happy with the outcomes of each timeline you think about; if you aren't, is it actually a wise decision? Likewise, if you aren't happy with all of the outcomes, then are you willing to take on that informed risk?

The rule lays out consequences and aftereffects in a very real and tangible manner and forces you to step back from your immediate emotion or impulse about a course of action or decision. It creates a mindset in which you articulate your short- and long-term goals before moving toward them. How do they play out and what ripple effects will they have?

The 10/10/10 rule impacts your range of choices because things that may seem important or easy to do now might not lead to either the small or big goals you want for the future. They might actually lead nowhere and just waste your time if you think through the appropriate 10/10/10 time periods. You might find that they are detrimental in a longer time period, and you were seduced into taking a short-term profit for a long-term loss.

When you apply the 10/10/10 rule, you train your mind to look at long-term implications. It is just as important for you to train your mind to look at your options and see whether they will advance you toward achieving your bigger goals. At the very least, you get a feel for the overall impact of the choice in front of you and whether it furthers your ultimate success or not.

It can impact the things you eat, the clothes you buy, the jobs you apply for, the people you spend time with, and obviously the business opportunities you wish to take advantage of. Many decisions take time to mature into their full consequences. Doing our language lesson today will likely not have any benefits for us tomorrow or in ten days' time. But if we keep it up, the benefits in ten years will be well worth it. If we only consider an hour or a day or a week in advance, we never give these actions their full weight and significance.

This exercise highlights what is truly important and what is not so consequential to you. Remove impulse and temptation from your life, and let discipline propel you forward. The 10/10/10 rule also teaches you to analyze delayed gratification. You might feel great about a decision in ten minutes, but you might feel terrible about it in ten days.

Or, you might feel terrible about a decision in the next ten minutes (maybe you have to have to break up with someone or push through a grueling workout), but you will certainly appreciate the outcome ten years later (i.e. by releasing yourself to be in a better relationship, and having a healthier body!). This rule allows you to remember that sometimes, outcomes of decisions play out over long periods, and a "good decision" may look different depending on *when* you look at it.

## Worldview

The second part of your mental checklist is literally a checklist of questions to ask yourself to make sure that you are actually making a wise choice for yourself. These questions make sure your decisions are aligned with your worldview, and they help you eliminate options right off the bat when you see that they don't fit in.

Again, these might not be entirely new concepts to you, but it's actually going through the motions that will set you apart from others and make your decisions as optimal as can be.

To make your decision, ask yourself these questions:

1. What are the main problems you are trying to solve? Can you solve them in any other way, either individually or together?
2. Do you have all the information necessary to make the best decision possible? If not, what information would you have in a perfect world?
3. Are any of the most important factors subject to change anytime soon? What realistic factors could instantly make you regret your decision?
4. What is the opportunity cost for this decision? In other words, what would you miss out on to take this current opportunity?
5. Does this get you closer to your overall pertinent goals? Or does it take you further away from them?
6. Are you making this decision out of a sense of duty and obligation or out of your actual free will?

When you get a sense of the answers to these questions, it becomes hard to lie to yourself or fool others into believing you. You run out of space to do something that isn't good for you when you articulate your motivations and reasoning. When you can "pass" all of these questions, it becomes clear that you are making the decision for yourself, because you want to, and with a clear purpose.

Going through this part of the checklist is like going through a mini polygraph (the lie detector test) test. It cuts through the chatter and makes clear what you want, even if it wasn't clear to you beforehand.

For example, maybe you're trying to make a big change and want to move to rural Spain and start life over again. You move through the questions:

*What are the main problems you are trying to solve? Can you solve them in any other way, either individually or together?*

Asking honestly (and putting your red Sigmund Freud hat on) you realize that you're craving excitement and more meaning in life, and hope that a move will bring this about, but you actually haven't considered less drastic ways to get the same result.

*Do you have all the information necessary to make the best decision possible? If not, what information would you have in a perfect world?*

Well, your friend moved to rural Spain and seems happy. Granted, that might not be quite enough information . . .

*Are any of the most important factors subject to change anytime soon? What realistic factors could instantly make you regret your decision?*

Asking yourself this you realize that two things give you pause—your boss may be o the brink of giving you a promotion and your brother may have a baby within the next year, who you wouldn't be able to visit if you moved so far away.

And so on. Now, these questions aren't designed to just deflate poorly thought out plans; despite discouraging answers, you may actually decide to move to Spain after all, but the questions and the perspective they force you to take encourage you to think more realistically about the move and take beneficial action.

## Boundaries

The third part of the mental checklist for optimal decisions is to set subjective boundaries for your decisions. A boundary can be thought of a decision you make once, so you don't have to constantly negotiate the same decisions over and over again. Having a boundary is not just an act of asserting your personal limitations and values, it's also away to save time and conserve mental energy. You don't' have to really think about a good boundary—it makes decisions for your automatically.

It's important to set these beforehand, because when you're in the heat of the moment, it's very difficult to think clearly and objectively. When you set them beforehand, as you can do while reading this chapter, you can control your impulses and emotional reactions better. You can think of boundaries as rules and hard guidelines for you to abide by. They help you limit your choices and can even allow you to come to a decision through a process of elimination.

For example, if you go on a shopping trip, you might decide on a spending limit. You can't buy a jacket for over one hundred dollars, or you can't spend over two hundred dollars total for the day. This is a specific metric that you can't exceed under any circumstances. It allows you to quickly eliminate options because you're simply limited to things under a certain amount. It narrows your scope based on predetermined requirements. Specific limits can help reduce your options because you can also set a limit on the number of options you even consider or a time limit on how long you have until you pull the trigger.

Another boundary is to name deal breakers or options that you will never consider based on a trait or characteristic. For example, if a car has a safety rating below a certain number, it's out of the question for you. Another example is to not visit cities that drop below a certain temperature. Deal breakers help you focus on what you prioritize and immediately avoid things you don't to save time.

A final type of boundary to help streamline your decision making is to apply criteria for your decisions. *I will only do it if it is X.*

Again, these are decided on beforehand so you aren't influenced by a lack of willpower or emotion. You can think of these as the opposite of deal breakers. If an option possesses this trait or characteristic, it is automatically your choice.

For example, you might only choose the best camera on the market below two hundred dollars. It would be your one trait to look for, and it would rule out every camera except two or three. At the very least, this excludes all of the bad options and leaves you a small subset that you would probably be happy with. At this point, you might even be able to pick randomly after applying one of these boundaries.

Another example is to only spend time pursuing a sales lead if it will be worth over five thousand dollars so you aren't wasting your time on something that would not amount to much. You could also only watch movies in theaters that have a certain ranking and ignore all others that fall below it. Finally, you could decide to not spend over fifteen dollars per restaurant meal, which would severely limit your choices.

Not only does this make your life easier by preemptively making sure your decisions fit into your life, but it also serves to limit decision fatigue. Recall that the ability to make decisions is not infinite and has a limited capacity due to the consumption of glucose in your brain. When you can apply these filters to many aspects of your life, especially trivial everyday decisions, you are able to save your mental resources for what really matters.

## Beyond Pros and Cons

The first method is to write a simple pros and cons list with a twist. This is actually a method American founding father Benjamin Franklin described in a letter dispensing advice on how to make intelligent decisions.

The typical pros and cons list works by listing what you would gain from a choice in one column and what you would lose from the decision in another column. Here's what a list might look like if you're contemplating eating pizza:

Pros: It's tasty, you satisfy cravings, you love cheese, it's in a nice part of the city, it's your cheat day, you'll feel happier after, you can save money

Cons: You are still trying to lose weight, you don't need it, you will binge on soda, too, you will feel gassy afterward

It's short and effective and helps you organize all the thoughts running through your head. You can categorize factors as simply positive or negative and see which side appears to have more than the other. It allows you to visually see your arguments instead of debating them mentally.

It gives you a way to analyze your choices based on what appears to be important. It also introduces the idea that you are making a decision about changing the status quo or not, which accurately reflects what you are actually deciding about. Make sure you are asking the right question.

Pros and cons lists highlight the importance of understanding what issues you face in making decisions. However, basic pros and cons lists break down in the face of more complex decisions than eating pizza or not. What if you are trying to analyze whether you should move to a new city or not?

What if you are trying to make a decision at work that has the potential to bring in two million in revenue—or not?

A simple pros and cons list breaks down in these situations because every factor appears to be the same and only counts for one. In other words, let's suppose you have a pro of making two million and a con of an increased commute by ten minutes. They obviously aren't equal in significance or magnitude, but in a simple pros and cons list, they would be because they take up the same amount of space: one line on a sheet of paper.

There's got to be a better way. How can we improve your old-fashioned pros and cons lists to be more effective and informative? We can do it by *quantifying* them. It can work in a few ways.

You'll still have a column each for positives and negatives that would occur if you engage in an action, but you will be assigning values on a scale of zero to ten to each argument that represents how important it is to you. For the previous example of revenue versus commute time, you would assign the revenue a value of ten, where the commute time might have a value of 1.5. The higher the score, the more important it is to you.

There are a couple of ways to look at the results. The first one is to simply decide in favor of whichever side's values add up to be higher. This is black and white. For example, if your pros add up to be seventy-four and your cons add up to seventy-five, you would choose in favor of the con and not partake in the act. This is a straightforward and direct approach, but many people will have difficulty with it if the results are close. Indeed, if you are choosing between moving to a new city versus staying put, perhaps you should have overwhelming reasons and evidence to do so; otherwise, there are not enough compelling reasons.

In this case, the second way to look at the results is to only act if the value of the pros list comes to be twice the value of the cons side. For example, if your pros add up to ninety but your cons add up to seventy, you probably shouldn't act, because there isn't strong enough reason to break your inertia and uproot yourself from the status quo. It's not worth it to expend the effort into learning new tasks and changing your lifestyle for a marginal gain of twenty value points, so to speak. This is an approach that favors the status quo because it realizes that motion is not always progress; sometimes it is just wasted effort.

The second method is what I personally prefer because I, like many people, am lazy. I don't want to do something that will require extra effort and work if it doesn't result in a significant gain for me.

If there isn't a clear, powerful reason for me to do something, why do it? In this way, I try to make decisions as binary as possible.

Is there a powerful reason that significantly overrides the negatives? If so, let it fly. If not, don't waste your effort unless you are seeking change for change's sake.

There are multiple standards of interpreting the results that your quantified pros and cons list produces: whichever is greater, if the pros side is twice as large as the cons, or any other arbitrary number differential that appeals to you. What matters is you are simultaneously finding your priorities as you assign values to everything.

There are also multiple ways to quantify the lists themselves. Instead of how important something might be to you, you can assign values based on the following:

- How much money it saves
- How much time it saves
- How close it gets you to a certain goal
- How happy it makes you
- How annoyed it makes you
- How much your significant other will care about it

This allows you to adapt your pros and cons list to the specifics of your situation, which is good practice in general. If you use generalized or abstract pros and cons arguments that are irrelevant to your situation or worldview, you will get an answer that doesn't accurately reflect your situation.

For example, suppose you are trying to decide whether to buy a new car or stick with the same car you've had for the last five years. Let's list the pros and cons quantified with how important the factor is to my happiness.

Pros:
- Feel better about self, 6
- Impress women more easily, 8
- Better mileage on commute, 3
- More comfortable leather, 8
- Better sound system, 8

Cons:
- Cost, 9
- Don't need it, 7
- Bad buying time right now, 8
- Would need to take a loan from parents, 6

- Higher insurance, 7

It's the act of going through and honestly assigning values to everything that also lets you find what is important to you. Some people might want a car because they figure it will be better for their commute, but when they honestly assess themselves, it might be just because they enjoy the ego boost a fancy car provides on a daily basis. And that's okay. Understanding what you're basing your decisions on is as important as the factors themselves.

Second, if you can understand what factors are important in your decisions, it allows you to see what you can address independently of the big decision itself. In this example, it appears that independent of the new car, the sound system and the leather seats appear to be very important. Instead of going all in on a new car, you can just address what bothers you about the current car and make a more efficient decision.

The last important factor in better, quantified pros and cons lists is to be aware of which factors are fixed and which are subject to change in the future. Your world may not be the same next year as it is today, much less tomorrow. The things on your list may change for better or worse. However, only some of those will change, while others are more or less static for all time. This is something to keep in mind because it means a con may not always be a con and a pro may not always be a pro. How much deviation are you willing to factor in and accept as time goes on?

For example, do you expect that you will always want a better sound system, or is that something that is in your mind right now because of a new coworker's influence? Differentiate between what can and cannot be changed at all, and make sure you aren't going into a decision with the idea that factors *will* change. That's like marrying someone depending on the fact that they will undergo a sex change. It's putting the cart before the horse in a major way.

Hopefully this can change the way you fundamentally look at pros and cons lists. They can be as complex as you wish.

## Satisficing

The next part of your mental checklist is to ask whether you are embodying this unfamiliar word or not. The word *satisfice* is a combination of the words *satisfy* and *suffice*. It's a term that Herbert Simon coined in the 1950s, and it represents what we should shoot for rather than something that is guaranteed to optimize and maximize our happiness. Perfection can be deadly in the decision-making process (as we'll explore a little more in a later chapter), but there are ways to moderate unrealistic expectations and keep our eye on moderate outcomes. After all, *enough* is just that—it's enough!

Generally, people can be split into those two categories: those who seek to satisfice a decision and those who seek to maximize a decision.

Let's suppose that you are shopping for a new bike. The maximizer would devote hours to researching their decision and evaluating as many options as possible. They would want to get the best one possible for their purposes and want to leave no stone unturned. They want one hundred percent satisfaction, despite the law of diminishing returns and the Pareto principle, which would warn against such measures.

By contrast, the safisficer is just shooting to be satisfied and for an option that suffices for their purposes. They want something that works well enough to make them satisfied and pleased but not overjoyed or ecstatic. They aim for *good enough* and stop once they find that.

These are very different scales, and for this reason, studies have shown that satisficers tend to be happier with their decisions while maximizers tend to keep agonizing and thinking about greener pastures after their decisions.

Maximization represents a conundrum in our modern age, because while it is more possible than at any point in human history to get exactly what you want, there is also the paradox of choice, which makes it impossible to be satisfied. On a practical matter, there are few decisions where we should strive to maximize our value. Sure, you want to take your time and make an effort when choosing a life partner, or picking out a permanent tattoo that's going to be visible to everyone for the rest of your life. But deciding what color socks to wear? You're better off with a decision that's not perfect, but good enough. Therefore, put forth *proportional* effort and just make a choice already.

Most of the time, you simply want something that is reliable and works. Suppose you are in a grocery store and you are trying to pick out the type of peanut butter you want. What should you shoot for here? Satisficing or maximizing? What are the opportunity costs of spending fifteen minutes ruminating over peanut butter? How much mental power did you waste reading the labels in detail, and what more significant future decisions have you undermined by blowing your cognitive budget for the day on this one decision? The same type of thinking should apply to ninety-nine percent of our daily decisions.

Otherwise, we are constantly overwhelmed and waste our mental bandwidth on maximizing where it doesn't matter and where there are massive diminishing returns. Whatever net benefit the most optimal type of peanut butter brings to your life is likely not worth the extra effort it took to find it.

It's unlikely that you're going to run to this chapter whenever you hit a fork in the road, but hopefully one or two lessons stick and you are able to make great decisions suited for you and no one else.

**Takeaways**:

- We are always battling our laziness in all aspects of life. With decisions, implementing a simple checklist of sorts can help.
- First, travel into the future with the 10/10/10 rule. This implores you to consider three different timelines in the future and how you'll feel about your decisions at those three points—that is, ten minutes, ten days, and ten months from now. Ideally, you want all three timelines to be positive; if not, can you live with the informed decision that one timeline might be negative or detrimental? This technique will help

135

you play out decisions in your mind, rather than focusing only on immediate results.

- Another mental check-in is to examine whether or not your options are in line with your worldview, and this is accomplished by asking a series of questions that both alleviate you of your blind spots and make clear the reasons you have for engaging in certain actions. There are few absolute, objectively good choices—rather, the right choice is the right choice for *us*, relative to our values and goals.
- Setting your own arbitrary boundaries can help with decisions because they narrow your options. This gives shape and structure to your decision-making process. You can set limits and use deal breakers or requirements—they all work to clarify your intentions and work more quickly.
- Look beyond pros and cons. Making pro and con lists is usually inaccurate and too subjective, since there's no way to weigh up each item, and we may be unconsciously biased one way or another.

- Are you satisficing or unknowingly trying to maximize every decision you make? Ninety-nine percent of daily decisions don't require maximization and suffer greatly from the law of diminishing returns. Satisficing, a combination of satisfaction and sufficing, is the key.

# Chapter 5. Decision Traps

In a previous chapter, we touched upon two of the biggest indicators of intelligent decision making: (1) understanding and working around decision fatigue and (2) avoiding stress and anxiety.

As if that wasn't enough, there are also literally hundreds of decisions traps, or cognitive biases, that can influence how you view a decision. Where the previous chapters were about you and your own filters, cognitive biases are specific flaws in logic or emotion that influence how you process the information right in front of your face. Information that could be plainly obvious to someone else might drive you in the opposite direction because of one of these cognitive decision biases.

The next two chapters might seem very obvious and familiar to you, and that's because you have probably fallen victim to their contents in the past. And you'd probably continue to fall victim to them in the future if they weren't pointed out to you.

Cognitive biases represent flaws in human thinking, whether logical or emotional in nature. They are conclusions that we leap to in the absence of, and sometimes in the face of, evidence that says otherwise. You can also think of them as a mental shortcut that seems to make sense at the time but falls apart under deeper scrutiny.

That said, it's very rare that we encounter such scrutiny, so most of us never realize we engage in these biases—and our decision quality suffers for it. They are a bit more complex than simply requiring more information. These are some of the ways our brains are fooled in everyday life.

For the purposes of illustration, I will be using the same example throughout the chapter: deciding between purchasing an expensive, brand-new car and a beat-up older car.

## Preferring Simplicity

The first cognitive bias is that humans tend to prefer simplicity. In fact, we believe that something is more accurate the simpler it is. By contrast, we also distrust more complex things. We trust them less and we even become suspicious of them because we feel that decisions should be simple and straightforward. Some decisions *can* be direct, but most of life cannot be reduced to a single question.

Wanting simplicity speaks to our need to avoid stress and anxiety in decision making. Juggling many complex options takes a lot of brain power and is quite stressful—in this state of mind, we might *want* the simplest choice to be the right one. That feeling of relief of not having to think about it anymore makes us feel that it's the right decision.

In our example, buying a shiny new car is the simple solution. We can trust that it's new, we can see the mileage, and we know it hasn't been crashed before by some shady past owner. We seemingly know what we are getting. We sign, we buy, and we take the car off the lot. It doesn't get simpler than that.

By contrast, buying an older, used car has exponentially more moving parts—moving parts that could go wrong and that might not be in sync with each other. There are too many factors outside of our control that we aren't able to judge accurately. We always have a sense of suspicion and distrust when buying a used car because we never know how the car has been treated and if we are being told the entire truth.

We prefer simplicity in all walks of life, and that means the decisions that seem the simplest or have the fewest number of moving parts are almost always going to be preferred. They feel more trustworthy, like everything is transparent.

This also implies another aspect of what we prefer—we prefer things that we understand easily and immediately. If we can't, then it's as though there is a logical disconnect and something is being hidden—never mind the fact that many concepts cannot be broken down in such a fashion, but that's why this is a cognitive bias.

Studies have dubbed this *cognitive fluency*—how easily information is digested and understood. If information is easier and more closely resembles a model you already understand and can make a comparison to, it will feel familiar and fluent as a result. For example, there is a science to branding and marketing such that studies have found easily pronounceable names and reproducible logos perform far better than others. It's the power of simplicity.

We would love to quickly be able to ascertain the major points of competing decisions, and if we can't, then we mentally write off the more complex version. Just because something is simpler at first glance doesn't mean you should fall for the chance to reduce your due diligence. Sometimes simplicity *is* better, but by itself it means nothing.

## Relying on Contrast

This cognitive bias can be seen very prominently in our example of buying cars. It's the error of being swayed by relative values. It occurs frequently when you make a comparison to something that doesn't matter yet creates a large contrast, which is not always the metric you should actually be considering.

Let's say the expensive new car you are looking at has a sticker price of fifty thousand dollars. The used car is only ten thousand dollars. However, the new car is currently discounted from the original price of ninety thousand dollars.

By simply introducing the relative discount, that sure makes it more attractive, doesn't it? Sometimes we will get caught in this trap of perceived value. It sounds like a good deal to get a ninety-thousand-dollar car for almost half off, but that assumes that the car is actually worth ninety thousand dollars and that fifty thousand dollars is also a fair price. By introducing the comparison to the number that isn't exactly relevant, one might actually feel that they're getting a steal at fifty thousand dollars.

However, this isn't considering the car on its own merits or its own absolute value. This is considering it only in comparison to something it shouldn't be compared to: a relative value which makes it appear attractive.

You are stuck on a fundamental misunderstanding of comparisons, not wanting to miss out on something versus evaluating something in a vacuum by itself. Life doesn't operate in a vacuum, but it's important to keep your focus on the factors that actually matter in your decisions.

In this example, the best course of action would be to judge if the car is actually worth fifty thousand dollars, despite how much of a discount the price represents. Then you can compare the absolute value of both the new and old cars at their respective price points to make a much better decision that is free of cognitive bias.

Otherwise, you just might be fooled into caring about something that is wholly irrelevant to what you are trying to accomplish. When battling the reliance on comparison cognitive bias, try to strip away the fancy trappings and focus on only one factor: the absolute, objective value.

## Avoid All Loss

We hate to lose things.

In fact, we hate to lose things so much that we often would rather not lose anything as opposed to gain a lot. This is referred to as loss aversion, and it perfectly encapsulates people's strong tendency to prefer avoiding loss as opposed to acquiring gains. We build our decisions around the irrational desire to prevent loss, even when it doesn't benefit us very much.

Even if there is a net negative effect from a decision to avoid loss, it psychologically *feels* better than a net positive gain. Emotions are not always useful in high decision quality.

Studies by Kahneman and Tversky showed that the motivation, and thus decisional influencing, of avoiding losses are twice as powerful as acquiring a gain. If your number one priority in decisions is to avoid loss, then what happens to the rest of the considerations, which are often more relevant and important? Out the window.

How does this fit into our example of dueling cars, one used and one new? A buyer will buy from whichever salesman is able to make the buyer feel like they own the car as quickly as possible—by putting them in the car, referring to it as theirs, signing papers, or making them otherwise feel emotionally attached. The salesman could even give the car to someone for a thirty-day free trial period, which would really cement the decision for the buyer. This creates the possibility for the feeling of loss we so wish to avoid.

Why is this? When someone gets familiar with a concept or object, especially in as tangible of a way as a thirty-day trial, they grow ownership. Only when you have ownership and attachment does the possibility of loss begin to matter. People usually react with irrational rage over even threatened losses. The act of mentally hearing, "It's yours, and I'm taking it away," has a greater effect than hearing, "It's here, and I'm taking it away."

How do you think you might react if you thought you had bought the car, only to have it taken away based on a legal technicality? It would be akin to physical pain to part with something you feel is yours.

Loss aversion is a powerful motivation for your decisions, and it causes people to ignore gains to prevent losses, playing it safe in a sense when it doesn't actually make sense.

For instance, a 2013 study by Cullen et al. found that first giving someone a reward and then threatening to take it away as a penalty was a far better motivational tool than handing out a reward after achievement. The fear of losing something that was already yours, having it ripped from your fingers, was far more powerful.

The pain of losing, or losing out on, something is more salient and raw than the joy from gaining something. We suddenly feel that we have been robbed, which is a stronger emotion than receiving a gift. However, just because the emotions are so disproportionally weighted doesn't mean the path of loss aversion is smarter. The decisions are still equal; negative emotions just tend to take hold on us more strongly and blind us with fear or rage.

Scenario A: I give you ten dollars, then flip a coin. If the coin lands on heads, I take the money back.

Scenario B: I flip a coin. If the coin is on heads, I give you ten dollars. Which do you prefer? Scenario B is clearly more comfortable psychologically.

It's not to say that you should ignore negative consequence in decisions. It's only to caution and gain awareness that negative consequences have the ability to take root firmly in our brains and never let go. They can emotionally color our perspectives until all we want to do is avoid a slight amount of potential negativity at the expense of a sure positive gain.

## Reduce Risk

Humans want to reduce risk whenever possible. This cognitive bias is about reducing the risk that you face in decisions—choosing the option that represents zero risk over something more lucrative that might have a slight increase in risk.

It is similar to the prior cognitive bias of loss aversion. We want to avoid losses because the emotion of loss is far more salient and painful than the emotion of gain, and it's the same with risk. The gut reaction of knowing you face a certain risk is far more powerful and convincing than the emotion for any marginal gain.

This is otherwise known as the zero-risk bias, and it's a cognitive bias that makes you prefer options where the primary goal is to eliminate one risk, where other options are actually better at reducing risk overall. That's an important distinction to make. We prefer one risk to be completely eliminated versus eliminating risk across the board.

A simple example of this is to imagine that there is a rowboat in the water with ten leaks in the hull. The zero-risk bias would focus solely on plugging five of the holes completely and reducing the risk from those down to zero, while the option of using buckets to scoop the water out doesn't actually solve those problems but is overall better for the boat's survival.

In a 1983 study by Baron et al., a questionnaire was given regarding a hypothetical cleanup scenario involving sites X and Y. Site X had eight cases of cancer annually, while site Y had four cases annually. One might suppose that site X was more dangerous and required more cleanup.

The questionnaire gave two general cleanup options:

1. Reduce the cancer cases by six between the two sites.
2. Reduce the cancer cases by five between the two sites and completely eliminate the cases at site Y.

A significant portion, though not a majority, of subjects ranked option two as better, even though that yielded a worse result overall. That's the zero-risk bias—when people are willing to completely eliminate one risk at the expense of lower efficacy and outcomes. This speaks to how humans prefer to face problems—the fewer the better, even if the fewer are more powerful and harmful. There is a preference on juggling fewer balls because it *just* feels better and safer.

See how our emotional sides are getting the best of us yet again? You can imagine how this affects your decision quality and clouds your judgment. More problems are bad, yes, but the number of problems in itself is meaningless to the overall decision quality.

How does this play out in our new versus old car example? You would be basing your decisions on which car completely solves one problem for you and ignoring any other considerations or aspects. This might be good if you choose to focus on something like safety, but we are usually more fixated on things like horsepower or sleekness. What we ignore is the overall satisfaction we would gain from the car in favor of having a car that solves one issue sufficiently for us. Reducing risk sacrifices psychological comfort for good decisions.

**"Resulting"**

This is when you focus exclusively on the outcome of a decision and, based on that, you act. It *sounds* so eminently reasonable, right? What else could you be thinking of when making a decision?

The reason this is a trap is because, for any short-term, single decision, the outcome is generally only loosely associated with the quality of the decision. Yes, the two *are* related, but perhaps not as strongly as we might think when we're busy weighing up options. When focusing exclusively on the outcome, we forget a crucial detail: that there are other things that determine the outcome outside of our action, a big one being chance and another being other people's actions.

For example, you might be trying to choose between two new prospective employees. Employee A has these pros and cons, employee B has those pros and cons. You sit down and consider these in detail, imagining what life in the workplace would be like if you hired each of them, and how that might play out for you. But you couldn't possibly know that employee B would eventually fall pregnant and leave or turn out to be an undercover double agent, or that employee B would have a life changing car accident and no longer be able work for you a week after being hired. It's these chance events that actually determine the outcome—your decision between A or B features relatively little.

That's the trouble with focusing on the outcome—we start to think that it's our decision alone how that outcome plays out. In retrospect, we might see that we were just one player in a complex wed of interconnections, but strangely, when thinking about the future, we can get tunnel vision and imagine that outcomes rest solely on what we do or don't do.

Luck plays a role, and always will. Luck can come in and completely demolish our informed guesses and hopes. It can come along and show us an aspect of the problem we hadn't considered before. It can merely change or modify the outcome we had anticipated. The point is that we simply don't know how much of an effect it will have on the outcome, if it has one at all.

It would be more accurate to think about a *range* of possible outcomes, rather than just one, and think of them not in terms of guarantees, but probabilities, i.e.: "If I do X, then there's a *high chance* Y will happen (but that chance is never one hundred percent)."

Another problem is that by focusing on results, we can lose sight of the fact that even if the quality of the decision and outcome *are* highly correlated, it may take some time for this to play out. You may make a good decision and not really feel it until months or years later—haven't you often thought something like, "Wow, I didn't know it at the time, but I'm so glad I did what I did three years ago"? Your decision may need to set others in motion, or the results may simply take a while to mature and come to fruition. Many people believe they made the wrong decision simply because they were expecting more immediate results.

We cannot use potential outcomes to help us determine the quality of decisions. The relationship is simply not that direct. But then what can we use? The decisions themselves, as we see them in the present.

Yes, we obviously have to keep in mind what we're trying to achieve by acting this way or that way, but we need to have wide margins for error and the effect of luck and chance. A decision needs to be considered in the here and now, with the information available to you, when measured against your goals. You need to constantly remind yourself to choose between options and decisions, rather than choosing between outcomes—which is a power none of us actually has.

Once you've made a decision, try to resist interpreting the results solely in terms of your own actions. It's human nature to try and see an outcome as our sole responsibility, but remember that it is actually a mix of your choices, other people's choices, and the unexpected impact of luck. You could have actually made a good decision that nevertheless led to a bad outcome for reasons outside your control. It would be a shame to assume then that this was a bad decision. Similarly, don't assume you've done the right thing just because things worked out in your favor. Many people end up with a lucky outcome despite making what is objectively a horrible decision!

## Confirmation Bias

This is the fancy way of saying we believe what we want to believe. Confirmation bias is the tendency to see, interpret, or seek information in a way to confirm our beliefs or preferences.

Ideally, all of our decisions would be based only on the evidence and facts. If you have an assumption, you test it and observe the evidence, and you adjust your assumption accordingly. However, it's hard to deny that whenever we have an idea stuck in our head, we often go out of our way to find a way to make it manifest. We're stubborn animals when we want to be, and it's a huge cognitive handicap.

Let's come back to our car dealerships. If you go into this process with the belief that only a certain brand of cars can be bought used, then you will see everything through that lens. It will serve as a given, or truth, for you. It's almost like evidence that sprang up from nothing but an errant thought in your head, or something you thought you read somewhere once.

You will search for information about that particular car brand and how it is indeed the only good used car. You'll ignore any evidence to the contrary as flawed or fake. You will interpret dubious information to be an exception or to actually prove your point in a backward way. If you believe you want to buy a Toyota, your research and analysis will only serve to confirm that belief.

This tells us two things. First, we want so much to be correct that we fool ourselves and ignore anything that tells us we're wrong. Apparently our egos need that on a daily basis even when we're not arguing with anyone else. Second, we just really, really hate being wrong, and we avoid that feeling by using the defense mechanism of confirmation bias. In either case, we are making suboptimal decisions.

A 1979 study by Snyder and Cantor even went so far as to show that confirmation bias affects not only how you interpret information, but also *what* you take in and absorb. Whatever the belief of the research participants was the information they were able to recall. They barely paid attention to information that contradicted their beliefs, as if it went in one ear and out the other. They literally created an echo chamber for themselves and maintained an environment where they were only surrounded by supporting facts and evidence. Someone else could read the same information and come away with an entirely different reality.

As you can see, confirmation bias is difficult to understand because its very nature is that it is not being detected. People are unaware they are ignoring contrary evidence; they just fixate on a particular stance or belief and commit to it prematurely.

Imagine that you decided when you were a teenager that you were destined to be a doctor, yet you discovered when you were in medical school that blood makes you faint. A strong confirmation bias would lead you to conclude that you happen to faint when blood is around because of other factors, and being around blood isn't even that important to being a doctor. Now, that doesn't sound right . . .

## Gambler's Fallacy

The gambler's fallacy is the feeling that there are predictable patterns in what are actually random sets of events. It's when you give far too much credit to the amount of control you can exert over the universe.

For example, if you roll dice, you might feel that you should eventually roll a seven because it's time for it to happen. Never mind the fact that this is not statistically or probabilistically sound, you are attempting to create order in something that is impossible to have control over. This is the cognitive quirk that makes humans superstitious, finding links and causal connections were there are none, or assuming that we understand the rules of a game governed only by randomness.

This is a cognitive bias that causes us to ignore the concept of probabilities and make a decision that makes zero logical sense. The gambler's fallacy is overall the notion that just because X happened, Y should happen, X shouldn't happen, or X should happen again. They are all, more often than not, independent of each other, and this should guide your decision making to be less biased. There is no causation, and just like a gambler thinks, "I'm due for a lucky hand at some point!" you will also think incorrectly.

For our car situation, the gambler's fallacy, or seeing patterns where there are none, makes a big difference. It will cause you to keep holding out for better models and lower prices on both the new and used car. This isn't something you can predict; you are simply trying to rely on a pattern that you've invented in your head that ultimately is incorrect. You have noticed what you perceived to be a pattern once, and the belief in that pattern is leading you down the wrong path. Each price that is associated with a new or used car for sale is independent of previous used car prices.

You are attempting to find logic and an explanation for a random series of events. There is no better illustration than how early mankind started to see entire scenes in the night sky in the form of constellations. The stars in the sky are certainly randomized, but there is the tendency to find patterns, make familiar, and put things into contexts we already know. Basing decisions only on verifiable evidence is what can put a stop to this cognitive bias.

## Rosy Retrospection

This is the tendency toward having far fonder memories than what actually occurred. The name comes from the saying of seeing events through rose-colored glasses.

We have the tendency to remember the past in terms of positivity. Why?

There are many possibilities. We consciously want to make ourselves feel better about our experiences and make it feel like we didn't waste our time. Because we want to be able to say that we're having fun and appear positive in front of other people. Because we subconsciously want to defend our sense of self and our actions.

A study in 1992 by Robert Sutton surveyed subjects who visited Disneyland and found that their actual experience was actually tiring, irritable, and expensive. Their expectations were not met, and some even felt like they had wasted their time. However, when the same subjects were surveyed after the trip to Disneyland, they universally reported the trip being more enjoyable and fun than they had in the moment. It was as if they had selective memory and chose to bypass encoding the negative moments into their brains and only focused on the positive.

What's interesting is that even though people tend to remember the positives of their experiences, research has shown that negative memories are actually more impactful and powerful. A 2001 study by John Cacioppo found that the brain has substantially greater activity in response to negative stimuli versus positive stimuli.

What does this all mean? Our decisions are constantly taken hostage by our faulty memories. We only think about the good when we use our experience as a factor in decision making. We should go back and think as deeply as we can about the negatives as well. You might have fond memories of a car of a certain brand because you learned to drive in it, when in reality it broke down every other week.

The memories, not the experiences themselves, call the shots. That in itself tells you how off-base our decisions can be. Even if you've gone through something, you have to make sure to consider, at the least, the average of the experience, not just the peaks and crests that represent the best of times. It wouldn't hurt to also remember the valleys and nadirs that represent the worst of times as a cautionary tale. Remember the Eeyore hat? Knowing that memories sometimes get a rosy glow, we can deliberately remind ourselves of how we actually felt during past memories to balance this bias. Finally, understanding this bias has a curious side effect: if we know that we tend to retrospectively decide that past events were better than they were, this actually means that we may have a greater chance of ultimately being satisfied with a decision we make right now!

Overall, decision traps and cognitive biases reveal one truth about human beings. We want to operate as if we are correct and understand the truth. This is highly positive and optimistic thinking, but it can also be called hubris and arrogance at the same time. It's not about becoming a perfect, flawless decision-making machine, but about becoming aware of how you are *actually* making decisions, so you can moderate your blind spots a little better.

How can you fight these biases from entering into your decision making? It's a matter of stepping back and first looking through these chapters to make sure you aren't committing grave sins. Honesty is key in this step. Slowing down and making the process deliberate and transparent is also important. Being unaware of what we're doing means all kinds of self-deceptions can come into play without us even realizing it.

To bring any potential biases out into the light, you must begin to ask yourself the following foundational questions that underlie your beliefs and reasoning:

1. Can you articulate your reasoning coherently without emotion or "hunches"?
2. How valid are the cons and arguments against your belief and reasoning?
3. What do you think influences your beliefs?
4. If all factors were equal, is this still the belief you would hold, or are you influenced by something external?
5. What do you gain and lose with this decision?

The moment you assume that you're thinking perfectly rationally and don't need to bother about cognitive biases, is precisely the time they're likely to trip you up! Cognitive biases and decision traps don't represent an occassional deviation from normal thinking—they *are* normal thinking. Keep that in mind the next time you think you are being clear-minded.

**Takeaways**:

- Through no fault of our own, there are many ways our brains can actively fool us into suboptimal decisions.

- The first cognitive bias is a preference for simplicity and a distrust for complexity. Sadly, life isn't always so simple. This can lead us to prefer the simpler, more direct option over options that are perceived to be more complex and have hidden factors.
- The second cognitive bias is a reliance on contrast and relative value. This makes us susceptible to terrible decisions because relative value is meaningless to us—the only thing that should matter is objective and absolute value.
- The third cognitive bias is a tendency to avoid losses. The psychological harm of a loss is exponentially that of the psychological benefit of a gain—thus, we seek to avoid losses in decisions whenever possible, even when it is illogical.
- The fourth cognitive bias is a tendency to reduce risk. This is similar to the tendency to avoid losses. We act to reduce risk because it feels psychologically more comfortable and less stressful, despite usually being a poorer decision overall.

- Cognitive biases are actually the most natural and instinctual way of thinking, which is bad news for your decision-making muscle. This chapter represents four more common cognitive biases that will cause suboptimal decisions.
- Confirmation bias is when you see or interpret things only to bolster your pre-existing assumptions and beliefs. This can cause, in a word, blindness.
- The gambler's fallacy is when you try to find patterns in random, chaotic events that you have no control over. There is a lack of using actual evidence.
- Rosy retrospection is when you emphasize the positive nature of a past experience and apply that incorrect assessment to a current situation. Your biased memory calls the shots here, not your wealth of past experiences.

## Chapter 6. How to Beat Analysis Paralysis and Indecision

For some of you, this might be the only important chapter of the book. How can you deal with indecision—the bane of so many people's lives?

Analysis paralysis isn't just a fancy, rhyming term. It's a real problem that can keep you from everything you hold dear in life, personal and professional. It's when, despite having all the information at your disposal, you are paralyzed. Perhaps it's *because* you have such a plethora of information, or perhaps it's because you don't actually know what is best for you. Regardless, you can't make a choice and you stall until you suffer the consequences for not taking action or until someone else throws their hands up in disgust and makes the decision for you.

Why do we have such an aversion to making decisions sometimes? Are we really frozen simply because of the paradox of choice? Interestingly enough, people who feel that they are indecisive aren't so in all aspects of life. It is usually confined to a certain area that they don't feel confident in.

This is one of the major reasons for indecision. When we make a decision, we are owning it and putting ourselves—our intelligence, creativity, fitness, musical talents, you name it—on the line for evaluation and judgment. For every positive reaction to a decision, there is a negative one, whether real or imagined. We absolutely hate the idea of being looked at in a negative manner, even if we're completely right. Making a decision opens you up to that can of worms, at least when you're making decisions for or in front of a group.

In other words, it doesn't usually come down to decision fatigue or trying to optimize for the best option, although it can certainly be an issue from time to time. The biggest reason most of us are indecisive is because we don't want people to think we're stupid. It's often a confidence issue as opposed to a pickiness issue.

For instance, let's take the all-too-common scenario of having to decide what restaurant to eat at with a friend. You might feel hesitant to choose a place because you feel like you're in a no-win situation. You want to please and accommodate them and make sure your choice of restaurant isn't judged. If you choose a place not to their liking, you imagine they will think you are both (1) stupid and (2) inconsiderate to their taste.

This in a nutshell illustrates the most common feeling of analysis paralysis. It sounds far-fetched, but when we make decisions outside of a vacuum and in the real world, your decisions say something about you to other people. If you feel like you can't win, you stay still in the hopes that you'll do less damage that way. At the very least, it can feel like an exhausting chore. That's where the instinct to dig your head into the sand like an ostrich can come from.

This notion is parallel to what we call "planning paralysis"—when planning becomes a higher priority than actually *doing* something. The job of *planning* to leave your comfort zone takes precedence over, or at least valuable time from, your actual project.

Planning and analyzing are comfort zones, not just because you can do it from a couch. To do something, you have to get outside and risk a certain vulnerability. So it's always easier to keep planning, because technically it's useful to your task. You can lead yourself to believe you're being productive toward making a decision.

Planning to map out precision and sewing up random details isn't the worst way to go about projects. But more likely, planning is a device that helps one avoid action to mollify our fears and anxieties. When we're spinning our wheels, it's because we've started listening to that inner voice that likes to harangue us into believing all we do will fail and we're foolish for trying.

Listen up, indecisive people and those of you who are struck with analysis paralysis. What follows are some tips for you to pull the trigger more quickly and confidently. You may have imagined you had to sacrifice one and you couldn't have both, but it's not true.

## Taking Action

It's called the paradox of choice: the more high quality information you have, the harder it seems to get out of research mode and actually *do* something about it. The term was first coined by psychologist Barry Schwartz to describe how having more options may give us a better outcome up to a point, but it usually comes with more indecision, i.e. analysis paralysis and the fear of making the wrong decision.

Think of a recent decision you made. How much time did you spend managing information around that choice? You might not have just lost time, but productivity and motivation, too. You see, mental energy is a resource that you can deplete—when you blow it all on overthinking, it's like you don't have much left over to actually *do* the

173

task itself. Overthinking tricks your brain into believing that it's helping you make better decisions—but beyond a certain point, there are diminishing returns.

You also lose out on creativity and spontaneity, which are linked. The more you think about what you're doing, the less you can relax into it and find creative solutions. Overthinking drains your willpower and leads to decision fatigue, i.e. agonizing over many tiny decisions eventually overwhelms you and leaves you too exhausted to properly think about the big decisions.

The negative effects are not just cognitive though. Economist Herman Simon distinguished between *satisficers* and *maximizers*. The former stop ruminating when a choice satisfies their criteria, whereas a maximizer keeps going, hoping to find a better and better option. Can you guess who is happier? Yup, the satisficers. Research shows that they also have greater self-esteem, better mood, less regret around their choices, and get less depressed. This is worth repeating: the "best" decision is often not the one you've stewed over for ages, but the one where you could say, "Good enough!"

The big difference is **taking action**. Here's how.

*Rank your decisions.* Don't fritter away time and energy on inconsequential decisions, but tackle the big decisions first, in the morning if possible. Ask if there are big decisions you can make that will make a ton of smaller ones redundant, i.e. saying no to a whole project spares you from saying yes or no to all the individual tasks it's made of. Don't make big decisions when you're tired or stressed.

There are a few ways to differentiate between the big decisions and the small ones. Ask yourself:

- How important is the choice?
- How will each decision affect you in six months, a year, five years?
- What is really at risk/what's the worst that could happen?

For very important decisions that will have lasting effects or high risks, take more time.

For less important decisions that won't impact the future much, you can safely wait a little to choose, or take a risk and just act.

*Automate with habit.* Willpower is drained away when you have to make conscious decisions all the time, but automatic habits take none of this effort. So, where you can, automate daily habits so they don't constantly draw on your energy and attention. Routines, the right software tools and good boundaries take many decisions out of your hands and leave your energy for things that matter more.

*Be a conscious information consumer.* Just because information is out there, doesn't mean you have to consider it. Information is unlimited; your attention isn't. Become a more discerning reader by deciding what your intention is *before* you read something—if it doesn't address this purpose, move on, quickly. Put hard limits on yourself, for example, if you say you're going to read ten reviews for a new purchase, stop at ten. You could also commit to considering only three projects per day; if something isn't relevant, ignore it till later.

*Set a deadline.* If we lived forever maybe considering every piece of information would be possible, but we don't. Give yourself a time limit on which to act. This will focus you and remind you that there are opportunity costs to dawdling and failing to act. This will also make you work more efficiently—is a task or piece of information really worth it, given the time you actually have?

*Stay focused.* An objective can cut down on rabbit holes and sidetracking. Yes, some ideas are important and interesting, but are they the *most* important and interesting, relatively speaking? Set some criteria for what is allowed to demand your attention. Does a certain task actually advance your agenda in a meaningful way? Keep this top of mind and you will be far less tempted by distractions. You don't have to pick apart every new option; simply ask if it's in the right direction with your main goals, or if it isn't.

Every decision has pros and cons, and you can go round and round with them forever. The one thing that can help you cut through all this is your own set of values, knowledge of your preferences, and your overall goals. There are no good or bad decisions, really, only those that fit *you*. If you have two very different but appealing seeming options, ask yourself—which one best addresses your highest priority in life?

*Get perspective.* Sometimes, what allows us to sink into analysis paralysis is getting stuck in our own heads and losing perspectives. Get another viewpoint from someone else—some research actually suggests that other people are as good or better at predicting which choices will make us happy. Ask a friend, mentor, coworker, etc. for their input, and put your case to them—sometimes just putting your thought process into words can shine a light on inconsistencies or gaps.

*Drop all-or-nothing thinking.* Very few decisions are life or death. If you think of them this way, the stakes seem higher and you deliberate more, twisting yourself in knots, digging deeper into a hole. But actually, we can do a lot to reduce our uncertainty by taking action and seeing what happens. What we think of as one decision can actually be many, and we can act, observe and adjust on each of these, considerably lowering the risk.

You can go a long way by simply omitting the wrong decisions. This is easier to do than finding the right one—you can find success eventually by just ensuring you're not failing where possible! You're a scientist taking many iterative steps, rather than trying to shoot one perfect shot, no second chances. Focus on the smallest step you can take that will give you some useful feedback—you got it, take action!

*Begin even when you're not one hundred percent ready.* It's often better to simply act, even if you're not feeling ready—after all, you may never truly feel ready. You may gain more confidence and insight by actually trying things out and learning any lessons you need to. You don't need perfect, complete information before you can make an educated guess. Analyzing can seem like a way to reduce anxiety, but taking action accomplishes this much sooner.

*Make the right decision—in retrospect.* A benefit of acting is that you put yourself in a new position from which to appraise things. You might be able to see that you're happy with even with a "bad" decision, and had been overemphasizing your own input in the final outcome. Even perfect planning doesn't guarantee success, does it? Another thing to consider is that it's everything that happens long after a decision that determines whether it's right or wrong. Many people believe the choice is a good one simply because they feel good about it, so they retroactively *make* their decision the right one, and work with it. In other words, simply committing to a choice is actually the thing that makes it work in the long run, and it becomes the right decision. So, commit.

*Aim for good enough*. No, not perfect. You might find perfection indirectly, but aiming for it usually just wastes time and makes you less efficient. Perfection comes at a high cost. Perfection is fragile and unrealistic. Moderation is key—a good enough decision is . . . well, good enough. Even if the decision *isn't* good enough, you still have something that the perfectionist doesn't have: lived experience to improve your next decision. All they have is conjecture and guesses.

*Forget your personal narratives around choices*. Over analysis can be a sign that we are trapped in old habitual ways of thinking, and allowing bad habit and past preconceptions color the present moment. Maybe you were taught that making a mistake was the worst thing in the world, or maybe you have some unconscious beliefs around being perfect. Perhaps you're still choosing according to someone else's idea of what's right. If you're stuck in paralysis, it's worth double checking that you're not letting inaccurate personal narratives trip you up.

## Letting Go of the Fear of Acting

First, realize that almost every decision is reversible and you can take them back to some degree. Therefore, it makes sense to dip your toe into one option to see what happens and gain some information instead of standing at the fork in the road until you starve to death. You learn so much more by acting as if you are going to take option B instead of hemming and hawing about both. It's only in the process of option B will you learn more about it and how it feels.

181

If you are trying to decide between moving to New York or Texas, are you going to gain more information by visiting neither and continuing to debate with yourself or by visiting one, seeing how you feel about it, and going through some motions to gain information? The point is that taking a few steps down one road is extremely reversible and worthwhile due to what you'll learn.

Second, as we discussed in an earlier chapter, apply strict boundaries to help you make the choice for you. It streamlines your process and reduces the amount of thinking you have to do. For example, if you are struggling with what restaurant to pick for dinner, you might apply filters of healthy, inexpensive, within a ten-minute drive, and not hamburgers. After you set these boundaries, you might only have one or two choices left over. It's like when you shop online and apply filters for size, style, price, and color; suddenly you're left with only two shirts to buy.

If you're left with zero choices, remove one or two filters and work backward until you can make an easy yet satisfactory choice. You'll be left with choices that are within your criteria, and at that point, what does it matter? You can choose at random at this point with no loss in happiness or effectiveness, and you've successfully ignored everything that you *don't* care about.

A corollary to setting boundaries is to first decide upon a *default choice* if you can't decide within a set amount of time. Pick your default upfront, then set a time limit, where if you can't choose something else, you automatically go with the default. For instance, with your significant other, your default restaurant is an Italian joint. If you can't choose a different restaurant within five minutes each night, then to Italy you go. This saves time, but the act of creating the default choice is important because you will have automatically selected something that fits your requirements or desires. You'll be happy in either case, in other words.

In many instances, the default is what you had in mind the entire time and where you were probably going to end up regardless of going through the motions and endless debate. You go through the mental exercise of choosing a "default" with the idea that you might end up there anyway.

Third, realize that you might have a drive to make the "perfect" decision. This is similar to what we've talked about previously with satisficing versus maximizing decisions, but it differs because perfection is about something that doesn't exist.

If something checks all your boxes, that's all you need to beat your indecision. When you aim for perfection, you also tend to start running up against the law of diminishing returns, which states that the amount of effort you put into something isn't worth the return you gain anymore. For example, you might spend a one hundred dollars on a pair of nice shoes. At that price point, they will be well constructed, sturdy, and fashionable. What if you were to spend two hundred dollars on a similar pair of shoes? They'd still be well constructed, sturdy, and fashionable.

This begs the question, were they worth the extra one hundred dollars over the cheaper pair? For most people, no. There is a law of diminishing returns where the more expensive shoes don't make a difference in any relevant way. How nice can a pair of shoes get? Unless the more expensive shoes are self-cleaning with automatic lacing, you are spending more for essentially the same return.

You probably aren't shooting for life-changing restaurants every night of the week. In this case, your compulsion to make a perfect choice is wasted energy. Eating is the goal, not choosing a perfect meal. Unless you are making life-impacting choices that you will feel the repercussions of for years, attempting to make a perfect choice is silly. The difference between the "perfect" choice and the "good enough" choice will be negligible, and you might not even feel it, or remember it, the next day. There won't be consequences that make a difference in the long-term, so what is the sense in spending additional time on it?

A famous comedian has clever input on this matter: "My rule is that if you have someone or something that gets seventy percent approval, you just do it, 'cause here's what happens. The fact that other options go away immediately brings your choice to eighty, because the pain of deciding is over." This is surprisingly similar to what former U.S. Secretary of State Colin Powell has to say on the matter, as discussed later in this chapter.

Fourth, to make better and quicker decisions, engage in intentionally judgmental thinking. This is the type of thinking you have probably tried to repress, but it will be very beneficial for your decision making. Think in black and white terms and reduce your decisions down to one to three main points.

Overgeneralize and don't look at the subtleties of your options. Willfully ignore the gray area and don't rationalize or justify statements by saying, "But . . ." or, "That's not *always* true . . ."

The idea is to focus on what really moves the needle for you and ignore things that, while they matter, aren't the most important things. Sometimes, consuming less information will help this because you are focused on a smaller set of factors.

Let's go back to the example of choosing a restaurant for dinner. How can you think more in black and white terms about something like this?

Simply reduce your restaurant choices down to what you might categorize as a first impression. Restaurant A is a place for burgers, despite the fact that there are five menu items that are not burgers. It doesn't matter—in black and white terms, it's a burger place.

Restaurant B is expensive, despite the fact that it has five items that are cheap. It doesn't matter—in black and white terms, it's expensive. Restaurant C is far away, despite the fact that if you hit good traffic, it's not too far. It doesn't matter—in black and white terms, it is far.

Seeing options in black and white terms basically generalizes their traits and removes their subtleties. Remember, if we're talking about destroying indecision, this is one of the best things you can do. If you have a hazy stereotype of your two options and the stakes are relatively low, then that's all the information you need.

A final method to be intentionally judgmental is to sum up your options in one short sentence only, no commas or addendums allowed. You aren't allowed to elaborate on anything. When you try this, you'll notice you can only end up with broad strokes, such as, "It's a burger place that's ten minutes away," versus, "Well, they serve burgers, but they also have lasagna and tacos. It's ten minutes away, but I think we can get there faster." Which one is going to be easier for you to ignore or accept?

## The 40–70 Rule

As promised, another corollary that relates to Louis C.K.'s statement that seventy percent is the golden number to hit.

Former U.S. Secretary of State Colin Powell has a rule of thumb about making decisions and coming to a point of action. He says that anytime you face a hard choice, you should have *no less* than forty percent and *no more* than seventy percent of the information you need to make that decision. In that range, you have enough information to make an informed choice but not so much intelligence that you lose your resolve and simply stay abreast of the situation.

If you have less than forty percent of the information you need, you're essentially shooting from the hip. You don't know quite enough to move forward and will probably make a lot of mistakes. Conversely, if you chase down more data until you get more than seventy percent of what you need (and it's unlikely that you'll truly need anything above this level), you could get overwhelmed and uncertain. The opportunity may have passed you by and someone else may have beaten you by starting already. The law of diminishing returns starts to hit hard at this point.

But in that sweet spot between forty and seventy percent, you have enough to go on and let your intuition guide your decisions. In the context of Colin Powell, this is where effective leaders are made: the ones who have instincts that point in the right direction are who will lead their organization to success.

For our purposes of making decisions, we can replace the word "information" with other factors: forty to seventy percent of experience, forty to seventy percent reading or learning, forty to seventy percent confidence, or forty to seventy percent of planning. While we're completing the task, we'll also be doing analyzing and planning on the fly, so this range of certainty helps us tend toward action.

When you try to achieve more than seventy percent information (or confidence, experience, etc.), your lack of speed can result in many negative consequences. It can also destroy your momentum or stem your interest, effectively meaning nothing's going to happen. There is a high likelihood of gaining nothing further from surpassing this threshold.

This way of thinking leads to more action than not. Making the decision before you're one hundred percent—or even halfway— ready to do so is the kind of move that kicks you into action.

Beating analysis paralysis in general is a matter of understanding why you feel mired among choices and taking perspective into account when you think about how much time you are spending deciding versus how much additional joy you'll receive. Setting boundaries to find essentially equal choices helps, as does seeing only in black and white.

**Takeaways**:

- Indecision is a tough beast to beat, but it's not always a matter of having the right tactics or avoiding the paradox of choice. Much of the time, we are indecisive because we are afraid of what our decisions will say about us to others. We are afraid of the judgment, plain and simple. Thus, we fall into analysis paralysis or planning paralysis.

- One method to beat indecision is to walk down one path, but to the extent that it is reversible. It gives you more information than you would have otherwise and forces action, which is the name of the game.

- You can also set boundaries or filters based on one or a few restrictions to help you get to a decision point more quickly. This can quickly turn your cornucopia of choices into a select few. Another application of filters is to choose a standing default choice, which you will use if you can't decide within a given amount of time.

- Being judgmental is bad, but being intentionally judgmental and painting with a broad stroke can make decisions much easier. This works by removing the subtleties and making you focus on one or two factors.

- Taking action is an obvious way to break out of analysis paralysis. Making a small decision give you feedback to work into better decisions. You can become better at taking action by abandoning perfection, setting deadlines and limits, asking for other perspectives, ranking decisions and staying focused on your priorities.

- The 40–70 rule is a final way of forcing action and a decision. It states that you should make a decision when you have no more than seventy percent of the information or gumption that you feel you need. Chances are that you are suffering from the law of diminishing returns at that point, and you know more than you need already.

**Summary Guide**

# CHAPTER 1. THE CORE OF DECISIONS: YOU

- Often, decisions can be consciously articulated. If you want Chinese food for dinner, that's easy to justify. But for both quicker and bigger decisions, you are likely more influenced by your subconscious than you realize. The importance of knowing potential subconscious influencing factors is thus extremely high to deciphering your actions.
- There are three models of subconscious needs and desires, the first of which is Maslow's hierarchy of needs. He articulates the following needs: physiological fulfillment (like food and shelter), safety, love and belonging, self-esteem, and self-actualization (a level which he claimed few people reach). Identifying your location in the hierarchy is identifying your

subconscious needs, which can then inform how you appraise different choices in life.

- By making these unconscious needs conscious, we give ourselves more clarity and control over the process of making decisions. Maslow's theory also reminds us that our needs can and do change over our lifetime, and we need to factor this in for longer term decisions.
- The next model is Tony Robbins's six needs: love and connection, certainty, uncertainty and variety, significance, contribution, and growth.
- Robbins believed that each of us is motivated to act by at most two of these needs, which guide how we act and what we value in the world.
- Unlike Maslow's hierarchy, these needs function like traits and are present in different quantities in people, as well as being expressed in endless different ways. Pinpoint your particular needs and understand your decision process better.
- There is nothing inherently better or worse about any of the levels in the hierarchy, or between the six fundamental needs. It's more about

discovering what is actually motivating you so that the decisions you make are satisfying your needs.

- Understanding your needs helps you discover your values and principles, ensuring the decisions you make fulfil you on a deeper level.
- A value is a rule, principle, or belief that gives meaning to your life. It is usually something you consider very important in life and base many of your decisions around. This is why when you're confused about what to do in a certain situation or circumstances that you find yourself in, the cause is usually a lack of clarity on what your real values are.
- The first step to discovering what your values are is to simply abandon all preconceived notions you have of who you are. Often, the values we have been living by are actually derived externally. This can be through our family, culture, historical era, etc. By starting from a clean slate, we avoid such influences from clouding our judgment regarding our true values.
- Next, think about the things that you feel most strongly about. This could be personal success, close family bonds,

serving others in the form of social work, etc. Finding one will often lead you to other values you hold because they point to a "higher" value you possess. Thus, valuing family over career means that your interpersonal relationships in general are valuable to you.

## CHAPTER 2. PRIMED FOR GOOD DECISIONS

- The concept of ego depletion is important because it leads directly to decision fatigue. With overuse, certain cognitive processes can flag and wane, in exactly the same way that muscles tire with extended exercise.
- When you reach decision fatigue, your decisions become incredibly suboptimal because you will either become paralyzed or make a rash, unresearched decision. Your willpower will perform weakly, in the same way that tired muscle is just not as strong when it's been working hard already.
- How can you preemptively deal with the effects of ego depletion and willpower fatigue? You can time your decisions

wisely such that they made only when rested such as in the morning or after a rest or a meal

- You can categorize the trivial daily decisions you have and make sure to only allot a trivial amount of time to them, drawing limits on how much attention you'll spend on inconsequential decisions. Ask what risks are attached to a decision, the impact it will have, and whether you'll care about it in a month's time.

- You can treat yourself like an athlete and make sure you are mentally tapering off in preparation of big decisions, you can give yourself more time than is necessary to reduce the role of stress and anxiety. Anxiety and low mood can color our decisions. Don't rush!

- You can also work on manipulating your transaction costs to make good decisions more of a default option, while bad decisions are more difficult.

- By automating as many decisions as possible, you take certain decisions out of your hands and get them done without you needing to spend any extra effort. Use tools, habits and routines to make good decisions automatic, saving your mental resources for those truly demanding decisions.

## CHAPTER 3. THE SIX HATS METHOD AND WRAP

- Most of us engage in very little with regards to our decisions. A pros and cons list, perhaps. But this still leaves us victims of your blind spots.
- The six hats method of decision making implores you to view a fork in the road from six distinct different perspectives. Typically these are represented by colors, but avatars are more illustrative. The six different perspectives to consider are Sherlock Holmes (gather information), Sigmund Freud (emotions), Eeyore the donkey (pessimist), a cheerleader (optimist), Pablo Picasso (creativity), and Henry Ford (information synthesis).
- The WRAP method was devised to specifically address blind spots. WRAP stands for widen your options, reality-test, attain distance, and prepare to be wrong. As you can see, these are not typical ways to approach a decision, though they can serve you well because

they represent what is likelier to happen in the real world.

- The 3P technique was created by poker player Annie Duke. It consists of preferences, payoffs and probabilities. Preferences refer to your goals and what you're actually hoping to achieve, payoffs are the potential benefits of different outcomes, and probabilities speaks to the confidence you have in certain predictions of the future. It's these informed predictions that allow us to make good decisions.

- The ICE scoring model also rests on considering three key components of any decision. The first is impact (the potential for you a choice, idea, action, or decision to serve your main life goals), the second is confidence (how sure you are that this outcome will follow your action, bearing in mind that luck and chance play a role), and ease (how easy it is to make the particular decision). A subjectively good decision is one in which has a high probability of having a high impact on your goals, whilst being easy to achieve. The bad decision is the opposite.

- There is overlap between ICE and 3P, and both have limitations, i.e. they depend on our accurate assessment of the three aspects!

## CHAPTER 4. MENTAL CHECKLIST

- We are always battling our laziness in all aspects of life. With decisions, implementing a simple checklist of sorts can help.
- First, travel into the future with the 10/10/10 rule. This implores you to consider three different timelines in the future and how you'll feel about your decisions at those three points—that is, ten minutes, ten days, and ten months from now. Ideally, you want all three timelines to be positive; if not, can you live with the informed decision that one timeline might be negative or detrimental? This technique will help you play out decisions in your mind, rather than focusing only on immediate results.
- Another mental check-in is to examine whether or not your options are in line with your worldview, and this is

accomplished by asking a series of questions that both alleviate you of your blind spots and make clear the reasons you have for engaging in certain actions. There are few absolute, objectively good choices—rather, the right choice is the right choice for *us*, relative to our values and goals.

- Setting your own arbitrary boundaries can help with decisions because they narrow your options. This gives shape and structure to your decision-making process. You can set limits and use deal breakers or requirements—they all work to clarify your intentions and work more quickly.

- Look beyond pros and cons. Making pro and con lists is usually inaccurate and too subjective, since there's no way to weigh up each item, and we may be unconsciously biased one way or another.

- Are you satisficing or unknowingly trying to maximize every decision you make? Ninety-nine percent of daily decisions don't require maximization and suffer greatly from the law of diminishing returns. Satisficing, a combination of satisfaction and sufficing, is the key.

## CHAPTER 5. DECISION TRAPS

- Through no fault of our own, there are many ways our brains can actively fool us into suboptimal decisions.
- The first cognitive bias is a preference for simplicity and a distrust for complexity. Sadly, life isn't always so simple. This can lead us to prefer the simpler, more direct option over options that are perceived to be more complex and have hidden factors.
- The second cognitive bias is a reliance on contrast and relative value. This makes us susceptible to terrible decisions because relative value is meaningless to us—the only thing that should matter is objective and absolute value.
- The third cognitive bias is a tendency to avoid losses. The psychological harm of a loss is exponentially that of the psychological benefit of a gain—thus, we seek to avoid losses in decisions

whenever possible, even when it is illogical.

- The fourth cognitive bias is a tendency to reduce risk. This is similar to the tendency to avoid losses. We act to reduce risk because it feels psychologically more comfortable and less stressful, despite usually being a poorer decision overall.
- Cognitive biases are actually the most natural and instinctual way of thinking, which is bad news for your decision-making muscle. This chapter represents four more common cognitive biases that will cause suboptimal decisions.
- Confirmation bias is when you see or interpret things only to bolster your pre-existing assumptions and beliefs. This can cause, in a word, blindness.
- The gambler's fallacy is when you try to find patterns in random, chaotic events that you have no control over. There is a lack of using actual evidence.
- Rosy retrospection is when you emphasize the positive nature of a past experience and apply that incorrect assessment to a current situation. Your biased memory calls the shots here, not your wealth of past experiences.

# CHAPTER 6. HOW TO BEAT ANALYSIS PARALYSIS AND INDECISION

- Indecision is a tough beast to beat, but it's not always a matter of having the right tactics or avoiding the paradox of choice. Much of the time, we are indecisive because we are afraid of what our decisions will say about us to others. We are afraid of the judgment, plain and simple. Thus, we fall into analysis paralysis or planning paralysis.

- One method to beat indecision is to walk down one path, but to the extent that it is reversible. It gives you more information than you would have otherwise and forces action, which is the name of the game.

- You can also set boundaries or filters based on one or a few restrictions to help you get to a decision point more quickly. This can quickly turn your cornucopia of choices into a select few. Another application of filters is to choose a standing default choice, which you will use if you can't decide within a given amount of time.

- Being judgmental is bad, but being intentionally judgmental and painting with a broad stroke can make decisions much easier. This works by removing the subtleties and making you focus on one or two factors.

- Taking action is an obvious way to break out of analysis paralysis. Making a small decision give you feedback to work into better decisions. You can become better at taking action by abandoning perfection, setting deadlines and limits, asking for other perspectives, ranking decisions and staying focused on your priorities.

- The 40–70 rule is a final way of forcing action and a decision. It states that you should make a decision when you have no more than seventy percent of the information or gumption that you feel you need. Chances are that you are suffering from the law of diminishing returns at that point, and you know more than you need already.

Manufactured by Amazon.ca
Bolton, ON